MONITORING PERFORMANCE

IMPLEMENTING A PLAN

INTRODUCTION

To be successful in today's competitive business world, managers must deliver results on time and within budget. By applying the processes, tools, and techniques shown in Project Management you will maximize performance and ensure optimum results every time. Suitable for managers at all levels, this book equips you with all the know-how you need to lead any project, large or small, to a successful conclusion. From starting a project with a flourish to motivating a team and overcoming problems; every aspect of professional project management is clearly explained. There is a step-by-step guide to project planning, while 101 tips offer further practical advice. Finally, a self-assessment exercise allows you to evaluate your ability as a project manager, helping you to improve your skills and your prospects for the future.

UNDERSTANDING THE BASICS

Project management provides structure, focus, flexibility, and control in the pursuit of results. Understand what running a project entails and how to improve the likelihood of success.

DEFINING PROJECTS

A project is a series of activities designed to achieve a specific outcome within a set budget and time-scale. Learn how to distinguish projects from everyday work and adopt the discipline of project management more widely to improve performance.

1 Greet a new project as an opportunity to develop your skills.

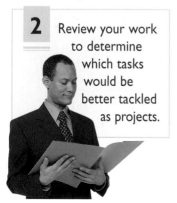

2 Review your work to determine which tasks would be better tackled as projects.

WHAT IS A PROJECT?

A project has clear start and end points, a defined set of objectives, and a sequence of activities in between. The activities need not be complex: painting the staff restaurant is as valid a project as building a bridge. You may be involved in a project without realizing it – for example, if you work in a special team, perhaps outside the normal business schedule, to a deadline. Routine work, on the other hand, is usually on-going, repetitive, and process-oriented. Some everyday work may lend itself to being managed as a project – tackling it as such will greatly increase your efficiency.

QUESTIONS TO ASK YOURSELF

Q What projects am I involved in at the moment?

Q Has my organization been trying to make changes that might be more likely to happen if tackled as a project?

Q Would I work more effectively if I regarded certain tasks as part of a project?

Q Could project management techniques help to make me more efficient?

WHY USE PROJECT MANAGEMENT?

In today's competitive business environment, a flexible and responsive approach to changing customer requirements is essential. Project management enables you to focus on priorities, track performance, overcome difficulties, and adapt to change. It gives you more control and provides proven tools and techniques to help you lead teams to reach objectives on time and within budget. Organizing activities into a project may be time-consuming initially, but in the long term it will save time, effort, and reduce the risk of failure.

IDENTIFYING THE KEY FEATURES OF PROJECTS

FEATURES	POINTS TO NOTE
DEFINED START AND END All projects have start-up and close-down stages.	● Some projects are repeated often, but they are not processes because they have clear start and end points. ● Routine work can be distinguished from projects because it is recurring, and there is no clear end to the process.
ORGANIZED PLAN A planned, methodical approach is used to meet project objectives.	● Good planning ensures a project is completed on time and within budget – having delivered the expected results. ● An effective plan provides a template that guides the project and details the work that needs to be done.
SEPARATE RESOURCES Projects are allocated time, people, and money on their own merits.	● Some projects operate outside the normal routine of business life, others within it – but they all require separate resources. ● Working within agreed resources is vital to success.
TEAMWORK Projects usually require a team of people to get the job done.	● Project teams take responsibility for and gain satisfaction from their own objectives, while contributing to the success of the organization as a whole. ● Projects offer new challenges and experiences for staff.
ESTABLISHED GOALS Projects bring results in terms of quality and/or performance.	● A project often results in a new way of working, or creates something that did not previously exist. ● Objectives must be identified for all those involved in the project.

EXAMINING KEY ROLES

Projects can involve a wide range of people with very different skills and backgrounds. However, there are several pivotal roles common to all projects, and it is important to understand the parts that each of these key people play.

3 Draw up a list of all the people who might be able to help you.

CULTURAL DIFFERENCES

North American projects need a senior sponsor to get off the ground and be accepted by stakeholders. Australia's flatter management structure means that projects also depend on senior support. In the UK, the sponsor can be at a lower level, provided that there is a strong business case for the project.

UNDERSTANDING ROLES

As project manager, you are in charge of the entire project. But you cannot succeed alone, and establishing good relations with other key players is vital. Important project people include the sponsor, who may also be your superior, and who provides backing (either financial or moral); key team members, who are responsible for the overall success of the project; part-time or less senior members, who nevertheless contribute to the plan, and experts or advisers with important roles. There will also be stakeholders, or people with an interest in the project, such as customers, suppliers, or executives in other parts of your organization.

INVOLVING STAKEHOLDERS

Aim to involve your stakeholders at an early stage. Not all stakeholders will be equally important, so identify those who could have a significant effect on the project; and when you draw up the project plan later, consider how regularly they should be consulted. When stakeholders are enthusiastic and strongly supportive of the project, seek their assistance in motivating others. Make sure that you forge strong alliances with those stakeholders who control the resources. Finally, check that everyone understands the reason for their involvement in the project and what its impact on them will be.

4 Build up a good rapport with your main stakeholders.

5 Make sure that your core team consists of people you really trust.

IDENTIFYING KEY PLAYERS AND THEIR ROLES

KEY PLAYER	ROLES
SPONSOR Initiates a project, adds to the team's authority, and is the most senior team member.	• Ensures that the project is of real relevance to the organization. • Helps in setting objectives and constraints. • Acts as an inspirational figurehead. • May provide resources.
PROJECT MANAGER Responsible for achieving the project's overall objectives and leading the project team.	• Produces a detailed plan of action. • Motivates and develops project team. • Communicates project information to stakeholders and other interested parties. • Monitors progress to keep project on track.
STAKEHOLDER Any other party who is interested in, or affected by, the outcome of the project.	• Contributes to various stages of the planning process by providing feedback. • Might only be involved from time to time. • May not be a stakeholder for the entire project if his or her contribution is complete.
KEY TEAM MEMBER Assists the project manager and provides the breadth of knowledge needed.	• Makes a major contribution in examining feasibility and planning a project. • Lends technical expertise when needed. • Is directly responsible for project being completed on time and within budget.
TEAM MEMBER Full or part-time person who has actions to carry out in the project plan.	• Takes responsibility for completing activities as set out in the project plan. • Fulfils a specialized role if involved as a consultant, or as an individual who is only needed for part of the project.
CUSTOMER Internal or external person who benefits from changes brought about by the project.	• Strongly influences the objectives of the project and how its success is measured. • Dictates how and when some activities are carried out. • Provides direction for the project manager.
SUPPLIER Provider of materials, products, or services needed to carry out the project.	• Can become very involved with, and supportive of, the project. • Delivers supplies on time and provides services or goods at a fixed cost, agreed with the project manager at the outset.

IDENTIFYING THE ESSENTIALS FOR SUCCESS

To achieve the desired outcome, a project must have defined and approved goals, a committed team, and a viable plan of action that can be altered to accommodate change. Abide by these essentials to keep you on course for success.

6 Make sure that people understand what you are aiming to achieve.

7 Ask colleagues to read your goals. If any comments are negative, revise the goals.

HAVING CLEAR GOALS

To be successful, a project must have clearly defined goals. These goals must be agreed by all involved, so that everyone proceeds with same expectations. The scope of the project must remain consistent so that it achieves what it set out to accomplish. Whoever agreed to the initiation of the project, usually the project sponsor or customer, should not need to make significant changes to its scope or extent. People who are key to the success of the project must commit their time to it, even if their involvement is only on a part-time basis.

GAINING COMMITMENT

A keen, skilled, and committed team is vital to the success of any project. To this end, the motivational and people management skills of the project manager are paramount. As project manager, it is your responsibility to develop the best team that you can, guide it in the right direction, and ensure that members benefit from the experience. Choose your team carefully and provide training, if necessary. The ongoing support of your superior, sponsor, and other interested parties must also be gained from the outset.

QUESTIONS TO ASK YOURSELF

Q Could I respond to a customer's demand by initiating a project?

Q Whom should I approach to get the project under way?

Q Am I confident that key people will lend their support to make this project successful?

Q Do the overall aims of the project seem achievable?

8 Expect to revise and enhance your project plan at least several times.

PLANNING AND COMMUNICATING

For a project to run smoothly, the resources required must be available at the time you need them. This demands effective front-end planning, taking into account not only people, but also facilities, equipment, and materials. A detailed, complete plan guides the project and is the document that communicates your overall objectives, activities, resource requirements, and schedules. It is also vital that you keep everyone involved fully informed of the plan and update them whenever it changes.

◀ **ACTING EARLY**

Check with your superior that a sufficient budget and realistic time-scale have been agreed for the project from the outset. This avoids the success of your project being threatened later because time or money has run out.

BEING FLEXIBLE

In a rapidly changing business environment, the ability to think ahead and anticipate can make the difference between achieving project objectives or not. You must be prepared to change your plans in a flexible and responsive way. It is unlikely that your original plan will be the one you follow all the way, since circumstances and requirements generally change as the project unfolds. This means that you will have to re-evaluate the plan regularly and adapt it accordingly. If your project is to succeed, you must be able to anticipate and recognize the need for change, implement it, and measure its impact effectively.

9 Learn to accept the inevitability of change.

10 You can hope for the best, but always plan for the worst.

DEFINING THE STAGES

There are five stages to a project: initiation, planning, motivating, monitoring, and closing. Start with a flourish, end positively, and recognize the different techniques and skills required to negotiate the three key stages in between.

 11 Make an issue of a new project so that people know it is happening.

POINTS TO REMEMBER

- A new project should be viewed as an exciting opportunity to bring new skills and knowledge to your organization.
- The team should be encouraged to build friendships and to help one another by making constructive suggestions.
- A system for recording what the team has learned should be established early on.

PLANNING A PROJECT

Whether you initiate a project yourself, or your manager or a customer suggests it, the first step in the planning process is to agree a vision of the project, stating exactly what it will achieve. To do this, you will bring together your core team members and people with a close interest in the project's result, known as stakeholders. Having defined a vision, you can identify objectives, agree on actions and resources, order and schedule tasks, and finally validate the plan with all concerned and gain their commitment to it.

IMPLEMENTING THE PLAN

The success of the implementation phase rests with the project team and, ultimately, your ability to lead them. You will have to think about team selection, understand how the team will develop as the project progresses, encourage teamwork, agree on key decisions, and adopt different leadership styles to inspire and motivate different personalities. To gain the commitment of all concerned, make sure that you start with a well-prepared flourish, using the authority of your sponsor, manager, and customer to focus everyone on the plan. You must ensure that everyone has access to key project information, and keep communication flowing at all times.

12 Monitor the project consistently from start to finish – problems can occur anywhere along the way.

MONITORING PERFORMANCE

Once the project is under way, you will need to assess how it is faring against objectives and time targets. An efficient monitoring system is vital if you are to deal with problems and changes before they throw a project off-course. During this stage, you will be asking for regular progress reports, organizing team meetings, and identifying milestones that will measure your progress. Once you have identified potential problems and threats, you can then use logical processes to overcome them, and to manage and incorporate changes to the plan when required. Finally, you will gain maximum benefit for your organization by recording your experiences for future reference.

Project manager greets new colleague with enthusiasm

UNDERSTANDING PROJECT DEVELOPMENT

> **Initiators of project agree a vision**
>
> **Key people outline project purpose and objectives**
>
> **Activities and resources are agreed and prioritized**
>
> **Project plan is approved by all involved**
>
> **Project manager executes plan, guiding team to achieve goals**
>
> **Progress is monitored and plan revised as necessary**
>
> **Project is successfully completed on time and within budget**

◀ MAKING AN IMPRESSION

Bring the project team together as early as possible to introduce them, and yourself, informally. It is important to start off on a good footing, so be positive and stress how much you are looking forward to working together as a team.

CHECKING FEASIBILITY

*Before starting on a project, you need
to be certain that there is a good
probability that it will be successful. Take
the relevant steps to find out whether a
project is appropriately timed, feasible, and
worthwhile before going ahead with it.*

13 Make sure you are
not undertaking a
task that cannot
be achieved.

14 Find out where a
project is in
danger of failure.

15 Examine whether
a given schedule
is realistic.

TIMING IT RIGHT

However promising and desirable a project may
seem, always examine carefully whether it is the
right time to initiate it. Take into account other
projects that have already started. Some
organizations have so many projects in place that
it is not possible for them all to succeed, so you
may have to consider postponing the new project
or curtailing those that are unlikely to produce
valuable results. Since all projects require access
to limited or even scarce resources, it is vital that
each has a clear reason for existing and that now
is definitely the right time for it to happen.

IDENTIFYING DRIVING RESOURCES

Every project is driven by the needs of the
organization. The stronger these driving forces,
the more likely the project is to succeed. If, for
example, a project involves winning back lost
customers, the driving force is very strong. To
create a list of driving forces, or reasons why your
project should go ahead, decide which business
concerns the project will have an impact on, and
then compare your project with other projects.
For example, if there is a driving force behind two
projects to increase sales, then the one that, say,
doubles sales is more likely to succeed.

QUESTIONS TO ASK YOURSELF

Q Are there any on-going
projects with a higher priority
than my own that are taking
up key resources?

Q Are my project goals in line
with the long-term objectives
of my organization?

Q How will the outcome of the
project affect the performance
of the organization?

Q Could this project damage the
chances of another project
being successful?

IDENTIFYING RESISTING FORCES

There are always reasons why projects may not be completed Such forces include people's resistance to change, the weight of the current workload, lack of information or resources, or a dearth of people with the necessary skills. Identify these resisting forces early on so that you can overcome them, or change the timing of the project. A strong resisting force emerges in organizations that frequently initiate projects to change the way people carry out their jobs but fail to see the projects through. If people view a project as simply another management initiative, it will take great skill to motivate them to make it happen.

▼ SEEKING EXPERT ADVICE

Ask a key team member with technical expertise to help you identify reasons why your project may not be successful. They may be able to pinpoint flaws that you had not previously considered.

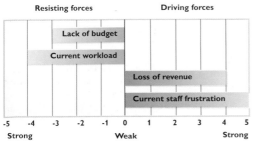

PREDICTING SUCCESS

A useful technique, known as forcefield analysis, will help you to decide whether the driving forces outweigh the resisting forces, and, consequently, whether the project has a good chance of success. By creating such an analysis, you will be able to see at a glance whether the balance is weighted towards success or failure. To assess the relative impact of each force, remember that drivers range from "one", a weak driver, to "five", an essential need. "Minus one" describes a resisting force that is not much of a threat to the success of the project, while "minus five" shows a force that is very strong, and that, unless you can minimize its impact, is likely to hinder you in achieving the desired project results.

▼ USING FORCEFIELD ANALYSIS

Create a simple diagram, such as the example below, to compare driving and resisting forces. List the driving forces against a vertical grid, and give each column a number between one and five. Do the same with the resisting forces but give them a negative measurement.

Resisting forces	Driving forces
Lack of budget	
Current workload	
	Loss of revenue
	Current staff frustration

-5   -4   -3   -2   -1   0   1   2   3   4   5

Strong   **Weak**   **Strong**

PRIORITIZING PROJECTS

When managing several projects, you must evaluate which is the most important to your organization in order to allocate time and resources. Seek advice from key people and use the discipline of a master schedule to prioritize effectively.

16 Put your projects in order now and avoid damaging conflicts later.

17 Check that project and organizational priorities align.

SETTING PRIORITIES ▼
In this example, the project manager is assigned several projects by her superior. By prioritizing effectively, she is able to complete all the projects successfully. A failure to prioritize, however, leads to disorganization, resulting in none of the projects achieving their intended value.

CONSIDERING VALUE

Before starting a new project, consider how many people and what resources it needs to meet its objectives. Your aim is to deploy the organization's resources to projects that offer the greatest value in their results. Discuss with your superior, and/or the project initiator, the relative importance of your project. You may wish to hold meetings with your customer or other project team members. The more complex the project, the more important it is to seek the opinion of others before you prioritize.

Project manager reviews projects but cannot decide which is most important

Project manager takes responsibility for three new projects

SCHEDULING PROJECTS

To help you decide early on how best to tackle a string of projects, create a form known as a master schedule. You need not identify all the resources in detail at this stage but write down an estimate. This will enable you to see where there are potential resource clashes between projects and confirm or deny the feasibility of a new project. If, for example, two projects require a crane at the same time, and you only have one available, you must reschedule one project to ensure that the crane is available for both.

Master Schedule

	JAN	FEB	MAR	APR	MAY	JUNE	JULY
Project 1							
Project 2							
Project 3							
RESOURCES							
Project manager	1	2	2	3	2	2	1
Engineers	2	4	4	5	4	1	0
Installation staff	0	3	3	4	2	2	1
Computers	3	5	5	7	4	3	2
Low loader	0	1	2	2	0	0	0
Heavy crane	0	0	1	2	0	0	0

▲ CREATING A MASTER SCHEDULE

Create a series of monthly (or, for complex projects, weekly) columns running to the right of the form. List all your ongoing projects and underneath, detail the resources (people, equipment, materials) you think you are likely to need.

Project manager seeks superior's opinion on which projects should take priority

Project manager falls behind with projects because she has failed to prioritize

Project manager completes all three projects successfully

THINGS TO DO

1. Decide which projects offer the greatest potential value to your organization.

2. If in doubt, seek advice from a superior or the project initiator.

3. Create a master schedule to outline the resources each project requires.

4. If available resources are in conflict, rethink priorities.

PLANNING A PROJECT

An effective plan maps out your project from start to finish, detailing what needs to be done, when, and how much it will cost. Prepare your plan well, and it will guide you to success.

DEFINING THE VISION

Having a clear idea of what a project will achieve is essential if you are to ensure that it will accomplish something of perceived value. With your key team members and sponsor, produce an overall statement that describes the project vision.

18 Be as ambitious as you can, but avoid committing to the impossible.

19 Create a precise vision to avoid ambiguous results.

20 See if others agree with your vision of the future.

DEFINING DESIRABLE CHANGE

Ensure that everyone knows exactly what a project is expected to attain by summarizing its aims. With your key team members and sponsor, create a statement that describes the project vision. For the statement to explain your proposal properly, it must answer the question, "what are we going to change and how?" Check the vision statement with your customers, who may help to refine it by describing what they would expect from such a project. If the project creates something of value for the customer that is a good indicator of its desirability.

EXAMINING THE IDEAL

To help you outline your vision, try to define what would be ideal. Start from a blank sheet of paper and ask the team to describe what, in an ideal world, the project would change. Avoid being held back by the situation as it is now. While you must remain realistic, you must also be creative in your thinking. Do not allow the way in which you have always done things to deter you from coming up with alternatives. If you involve the customer in this process, avoid giving them the impression that this is how the world will be, but how you would like it to be. Check how feasible the ideal is to arrive at your vision.

CREATING A PROJECT VISION

Identify a need
for change

Meet with key team
members and sponsor

Define what the project
would ideally change

Assess the likelihood of
attaining ideal vision

Produce a feasible
vision statement

DO'S AND DON'TS

✔ Do compromise on the ideal if that is what it takes to arrive at the vision.

✔ Do make the vision statement explain why the project is needed.

✘ Don't ignore obstacles at this stage – they may prove to be major stumbling blocks.

✘ Don't involve too many people this early in the process.

AGREEING A VISION ▶
Encourage team members to question every aspect of the vision to check that it is truly workable and achievable. Make sure that everyone agrees on the way ahead, so that they are committed to attaining the vision.

21 Check at this stage that the vision is clearly worth attaining.

SETTING OBJECTIVES

O nce you have agreed the project vision, you must set clear objectives that will measure the progress and ultimate success of the project. Expand the vision to clarify the purpose of the project, list the objectives, and then set priorities and interim targets.

22 Gain agreement on objectives from everyone involved in the project.

23 Make sure that your objectives are measurable.

24 Think how relevant an objective will be when it is achieved.

DEFINING PURPOSE

Expand the vision statement to explain what you are going to do, how long it will take, and how much it will cost. Your statement of purpose should reflect the relative importance of time, cost, and performance. For example, if you aim to create a product that competes with the newest solutions available, the key purpose is performance. Time-scale is the key driver if you must install a new system before starting international operations. Cost is the key purpose if you cannot, under any circumstances, spend more than last year's budget.

DEFINING OBJECTIVES AND INDICATORS

List the specific objectives you wish to achieve, covering the areas of change that the project involves. Avoid listing an activity, such as "complete a pilot", instead of an objective, which would be to "demonstrate that the project will achieve the planned business impact". Ensure that progress against objectives is measurable by setting an "indicator" against each one. For example, if your objective is to increase sales of a new drink, use the indicator of sales volume to measure success. If you are having difficulty in arriving at the indicator, ask the question, "How will we know if we have achieved this objective?"

▼ RESEARCHING STANDARDS

Nominate a team member to read up on industry standards. These will provide a benchmark for your own indicators and check on your competitiveness.

Team member studies competitors' brochures

SETTING PRIORITIES AND TARGETS

It is unlikely that all the objectives will be equally important to your organization. Give each a priority of one to ten, where one is the least important. It will probably be obvious which objectives are significant and which are not, but priorities of those falling in between will be less clear. Discuss and agree these with the team. Then set targets. These may be simple, such as increasing sales by 50 per cent, or they may be more complex. If, for example, your objective is to improve customer satisfaction, and the indicator is based on complaints, you must count the number of complaints you now receive, and set a target for reducing them.

▼ DECIDING ON PROJECT EMPHASIS

Write down your objectives, indicators, priorities, current performance, and targets. This will help you to decide which aspects of the project require most effort and resources.

POINTS TO REMEMBER

● Objectives should be always be appropriate for the whole organization, not just your own area or department.

● It will be easier to identify targets if you discuss them with others, including your customers.

● Well-defined and appropriate targets will enthuse and motivate team members, encouraging good team morale.

> **25** Be prepared to drop any objective that has a low priority.

Key objectives that determine project's success

Priority of objective

Objective	Indicator	P	Current	Target
Improve sales of non-standard products	Increase volume of orders	10	5 million	7.5 million
Improve the speed of decision-making	Reduce time taken to respond to a customer request for a quotation	8	8 weeks	4 weeks
Improve efficiency of preparing customer quotations	(a) Reduce time spent on preparing quotations (b) Cut number of days spent on product training courses	6	(a) 4 days per month (b) 5 days per year	(a) 2 days per month (b) 0 days per year
Improve management accountability for proposals	Make a single manager accountable for producing each customer proposal	6	Not done	In place

Measure of the objective's success

Current level of performance

Desired level of performance

ASSESSING CONSTRAINTS

Every project faces constraints, such as limits on time or money. Occasionally, such constraints may even render the project unfeasible. Make sure that team members understand the constraints in advance, and that they are able to work within them.

> **26** You can overcome most constraints by planning how to get around them.

▼ LIMITING CHANGE

Talk through any changes you wish to make with your superior, but be prepared to accept that some will not be approved. There may be valid reasons for keeping certain processes or practices intact.

PROTECTING WHAT WORKS

There is little point in change for the sake of it if you can work within the constraints of what currently exists. Even if you identify an area for improvement, it may be better to include the change in a later project, rather than deal with it immediately. This is because too many changes can put a project at risk as people try to cope with too fluid an environment. Also, by taking on too many changes, there is the danger that you will not be able to identify those that have resulted in the success of the project, or indeed, its failure.

ASSESSING TIME CONSTRAINTS

A fast-moving business environment often gives projects a specific window of opportunity. If you are facing a competitor who is to deliver a new product into the shops for the autumn season, you must work within that time constraint. You will not benefit from working hard to deliver a competitive product if you cannot launch the new range in time for your customers to place orders. Whether you like it or not, the time constraint has been set and you must work within that boundary.

> **27** Face up to constraints in a logical fashion.

> **28** Do your best to find short cuts to success.

EXAMINING RESOURCE LIMITATIONS

Most organizations work within limited resources and budgets, and projects are subject to similar constraints. A new project may entail an extravagant use of resources, so you will need to make sure that they really would be available. But if the success of your project depends on a level of resources that is unlikely to be forthcoming, think again, and alter the objectives of the project. For example, if you can complete the project with fewer resources, then you should make that your plan. Alternatively, if you are in a position to negotiate for more time and money to enable the project to go ahead, do so.

THINGS TO DO

1. Assess whether time is of the essence.

2. Analyze what resources you will need and whether you can afford them.

3. Look into using existing processes or resources.

4. Identify any external constraints, such as legal or environmental regulations.

5. Decide whether to proceed within the given constraints.

29 Explain the constraints to all who agree to take part in the project.

USING EXISTING PROCESSES

In order to reduce project time-scales, look at what currently exists. For example, other departments may have plans for change in an associated area that you could capitalize on, product parts that would shortcut design, or current technologies that would avoid the need to invent something new. It is important to consider these issues and reuse as much as possible. It is rarely a good idea to start from scratch, no matter how appealing that may seem.

CASE STUDY

Robert was asked to create a Web site for his department. Since he did not have the expertise to do this alone, he asked two outside companies that specialized in setting up and maintaining Web sites to quote for the work.

Robert's sponsor thought that both quotations were too high, and advised Robert to look at the Web sites already created by other departments within their organization.

Robert particularly liked the site designed and maintained by Anne-Marie, who showed him how to use the software she had bought in especially to create her site.

As a result, Robert was able to create the Web site for his department. In doing so, he not only saved the money that had been allocated specifically for that purpose but also made further use of the software investment originally made by Anne-Marie.

◀ CAPITALIZING ON INVESTMENTS

By studying systems in other departments within your organization, you can capitalize on internal expertise and experience, at the same time saving your organization money.

LISTING ACTIVITIES

Having identified your objectives and constraints, you can now plan in greater detail. List all the activities needed to achieve the objectives and divide them into groups to make it easier to assess what must be done, when, and by whom.

30 Make sure that you consult widely when creating your activity list.

WHY LIST ACTIVITIES?

Breaking the project work down into smaller units, or activities, makes it much easier to see how work overlaps, and how some activities may affect the timing or outcome of others. Since the list can be long, it helps to divide activities into groups so that each set of tasks becomes more manageable and easier to track when monitoring performance and progress. Grouping activities also helps you determine how they fit into a logical sequence for completion, which aids scheduling and enables you to assess the number of people and the skills that will be needed. Listing activities in this way also reduces the risk of misunderstandings, since everyone knows what their tasks are.

Team member records each activity on a flip chart

Team member with experience of similar project lends experience to the brainstorm

31 Try to describe each activity within a short sentence or two.

DRAWING UP A LIST

Start the process by brainstorming a list of activities. You may need to include more people at this stage. It is often useful, for example, to ask various stakeholders for their views on what it will take to complete the project, especially if it is a complex one. You may also wish to consult other potential team members. Such consultation makes sensible use of other people's expertise and experience. Ideally, if someone in the organization has previously completed a similar project, consult the original project manager and use the previous plan as a checklist. At this stage it is not necessary to concern yourself with the order in which the activities will occur; this comes later.

32 Keep checking your list to see if anything is missing.

PLANNING PROJECT ACTIVITIES

Brainstorm a comprehensive list

Group activities into a logical order

Check that nothing has been missed

Give each group and activity a unique identifying number

Document the activity list

Project manager guides team but does not judge contributions

Team member feels free to suggest an activity

Colleague is aware that this is not the time to pass comment

◀ **BRAINSTORMING ACTIVITIES**
Use a brainstorming session to generate ideas on all the activities needed to complete the project. Note every activity suggested, no matter how inconsequential. Your aim is to draw up a comprehensive list that can be refined later.

GROUPING ACTIVITIES

Break down your long list of activities into smaller, more manageable units by putting the activities into logical groups. You can ask the team to help you or, as project manager, you can do it yourself. Most groups will be obvious. Perhaps certain activities are all concerned with one event occurring later in the project, or some may all involve the same department or people with similar skills. If an activity does not fit into a group, question whether it is really necessary, or leave it as a separate entity.

33 Present your activity list so that it is clear and easy to understand.

GROUPING ACTIVITIES ▶

To group activities effectively, consider the logical order in which they will have to happen. One group, for example, may not be able to start before another is complete. The extract shown lists groups of activities involved in bringing a new product to the manufacturing stage.

34 Ask specialists for advice when grouping activities.

35 Put the list away and review it a week later with a fresh perspective.

ACTIVITIES AND GROUPS

1 **Conduct analysis**
   1.1 Interview customer representatives
   1.2 Consolidate findings into a report
   1.3 Present report to board
2 **Agree product outline**
   2.1 Hold discussions with departments
   2.2 Gain budget approval
3 **Complete design**
   3.1 Take first draft to representative customers
   3.2 Amend to answer customer comments
   3.3 Gain top level agreement to design
4 **Arrange logistics**
   4.1 Order materials
   4.2 Train personnel
   4.3 Engage sub-contractors

IDENTIFYING TYPICAL GROUPS

Every project has a start-up phase, or a group of activities that signifies the launch of the project, introduces team members, and records what each person has committed to achieving. Similarly, there should be a group of activities marking the project's close-down, involving final checks on performance indicators and finalizing project records for the benefit of subsequent project managers. Finally, most projects need a group of communications activities, for example issuing weekly progress reports or holding a presentation shortly before a planned pilot scheme goes live.

CHECKING FOR GAPS

Review your list of activities and groups to ensure that it is complete. If you miss out this step now and realize later that you have overlooked something, it could have serious implications on the project's budget, schedule, or other resources. Have you identified every activity needed in each group? Go through the planned activities step-by-step: is there anything missing; are you assuming that something will have happened in between activities that you have not actually listed? Once you are confident that each group is complete, give each group and each activity within the group a unique identifying number.

QUESTIONS TO ASK YOURSELF

Q If we complete all the activities listed, will we have done everything required to meet the project's objectives?

Q Will the activities ensure that we hit our indicator targets?

Q Does our activity list reflect the priorities we originally set for each objective?

Q Have we written down all our activities in sufficient detail?

Q Are all of the activities listed really necessary?

PLANNING A PILOT

Another group of activities that features in many projects, especially when the purpose is to create something entirely new, is a pilot implementation. Typical activities include choosing a limited number of people as a pilot team, implementing the whole project on a limited basis, and keeping records of the experience. By building a pilot phase into the plan, you will have a far less stressful and error-prone time when it comes to rolling out the entire project.

Choose your people for the pilot scheme carefully and make them aware that they are, for this particular project, guinea pigs. Make sure you communicate your thanks to them after the project, since their agreement to be involved at an early stage probably caused them some problems.

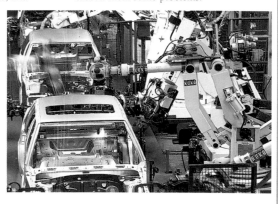

RUNNING A TRIAL ▶
Testing a new idea, even one as complex as an automated production line, allows problems to be solved before a new system is introduced more widely.

COMMITTING RESOURCES

Before starting to implement a project, you must study resource requirements and budgets. The feasibility of the project depends on you and your team being able to justify the expenditure by comparing it favourably with the proposed benefits.

36 Estimate costs carefully – once approved, you are bound by them.

ESTIMATING MANPOWER

Think about who needs to be involved in each activity and for how long in actual man days. A team member may need to work on a project for a period of ten days, but if he or she has to work on it for only 30 minutes per day, the total commitment is just five hours. If the member can usefully work on other projects for the rest of the time, the cost to your project will be a fraction of the member's ten-day earnings or charge. But if he or she can make no contribution elsewhere, then your project's budget must bear the full cost.

37 Provide the best supplies, facilities, and equipment you can afford.

CONSIDERING KEY RESOURCES

PEOPLE

How many people do you need? — Assess who will take on each activity

What type of skills do they require? — Identify levels of expertise required

OTHER RESOURCES

Are facilities, materials, or supplies essential? — Look at what each activity requires

Is information or technology needed? — Examine using existing systems

MONEY

What is the total cost of project? — Consider the cost of all the resources

Are sufficient funds available? — Check the budget that was agreed

IDENTIFYING OTHER RESOURCES

While the major cost of a project is generally the people, there are other resources that will have an impact on the budget. For example, you may have to commission market research. Facilities, equipment, and materials may also involve expenditure. Failure to identify all the costs will mean that you lose credibility when others examine the project to balance its costs against its benefits. A comprehensive estimate of costs at this stage also reduces the risk that you will have to request extra funds once the project is up and running.

38 Ensure that the budget will allow you to complete all your activities.

EXAMINING THE DETAILS

It is not enough to know that the team will need a training room for a month during the project, you will also need to know how large that room needs to be and what kind of equipment you should install in it. The better the detail at this stage, the more likely you are to avoid problems during the implementation. This will enable your team to focus on achieving objectives rather than on fixing matters that were poorly planned.

CHOOSING A COSTING METHOD

Whatever resources you consider, you can calculate their cost in one of two ways: absolute costing or marginal costing. Absolute costing means calculating the exact cost of the resource. If, for example, a new computer is essential for the project, the amount you pay for it becomes a project cost. If you can use an existing computer, allocate a proportion of its cost to the project. Marginal costing means that you only allocate costs to the project if they would not be incurred if the project did not take place. For example, if an existing computer, which is not being used, is required, the marginal, or extra cost, of the computer is nil. The cost of the computer should not be in the project budget. With practice, marginal costing is easy to calculate and is generally a more accurate measure of the cost of a project to an organization.

MAKING COMPROMISES

In an ideal world, you would gain approval for all the resources you need. In reality, you will probably have to cope with less. The person you most want for a certain task may be unavailable, or the best premises for the project occupied, and you will have to make compromises. Look for compromises that will not threaten the overall aims and objectives of the project. For example, you may be able to recruit a highly skilled worker part-time and allocate the remainder of the work to a less experienced, yet able, team member.

39 Avoid cutting back on tools that the team really need.

40 If resources are scarce, consider your alternatives.

 41 Refine a resource plan until anyone could work from it.

CREATING A ▼ COMMITMENT MATRIX
When you have identified all the resources and estimated costs, document these on a commitment matrix and seek your stakeholders' agreement to it.

DOCUMENTING RESOURCES

The key to ensuring that the resources you require will be available when you need them is to produce a document that all the stakeholders can agree to. This is known as a commitment matrix, because it can be used to remind people of their commitments. Check that the matrix is complete and that every group of activities is comprehensive so that you can be sure that you have identified all the necessary resources.

Activity as identified by number on activity list

Team members assigned to carry out activity

Resources required to carry out activity

Total cost involved

Activity	People			Resources			Cost
	Who responsible	Who involved	Training needs	Facilities	Equipment	Materials	
2.1	AJB (2 days)	RHC (5 days)	Interview techniques (1 day)	Meeting room Syndicate rooms (2)	OHP (1) Chart (1) Computer (1 day)	Market research report	£23,500

USING OUTSIDE RESOURCES

While many resources will come from within your team or organization, you will need to go outside for others. Make sure that you get competitive quotations from potential suppliers and reach an agreement on costs and performance that makes it easy for both parties to monitor progress tightly. You may need to brush up on your negotiating skills beforehand to ensure that you can win the best deal. While it may seem unnecessary to go into such detail at the outset, the tighter the agreement, the more likely you are to avoid conflict.

MAKING CONTACTS ▶
Ensure that you meet with several potential suppliers and keep their details on record. Even if you decide not to use them this time, an extensive network of contacts could well prove useful for future projects.

GETTING SIGN-OFF

Before you can obtain the official go-ahead for a new project, it must be proven that it is still a business priority and that its benefits to the organization considerably outweigh its costs. This is known as investment appraisal, or cost-benefit analysis, and it is a discipline used widely in many organizations which often have formal systems for the process. If the costs are the same or more than the benefits, the sponsors have three alternatives: they can proceed with the project regardless (although this is seldom desirable unless the strategic value of the project is very important to the long-term aims of the organization); they can modify the objectives and change the activities in a way that reduces costs; or they can cancel the project because it is considered unfeasible.

POINTS TO REMEMBER

● If your organization has an official system for obtaining sign-off for a project, this should be followed.

● Finance departments can provide useful feedback on your estimates by comparing your project's costs with others.

● The benefits of a project should never be exaggerated – promises will be expected to be delivered.

42 Be prepared to justify your choices, dates, and budgets.

ORDERING ACTIVITIES

Not all activities can, or need, to start at the same time to meet the project's planned completion date. Put activities into a logical sequence, estimate the duration of each, and then use clear documentation to help you devise a project schedule.

43 Remember that activities can be carried out in parallel.

44 Ask whoever is responsible for an activity to give you their estimated start and end dates.

CONSIDERING ORDER

Having completed a list of the activities required to complete the project, look at how they inter-relate. Decide which activities should start immediately or first, which need to be completed before moving on to the next, and work through all the activities until the end of the project. Some activities will be the culmination of a number of others. For example, the team will probably need to complete several activities before it can make a presentation to the people involved in a pilot scheme. Important activities will be review meetings.

ESTIMATING ACTIVITY TIMES

To draw up an effective schedule, you need to know how much time each activity is likely to take. It is important to estimate these durations accurately, since poor guesswork may throw the entire project off course. Team members should also have input to ensure that they agree with the estimated activity times and will be able to work to the schedule that you produce. If there is major doubt as to how long an activity could take, estimate best and worst case scenarios and work out a compromise between the two. If a project is under time pressure this will help to identify where you could reduce the overall time-scale.

QUESTIONS TO ASK YOURSELF

Q Do I have time to do a trial run of an activity to test how long it might take?

Q Could I estimate the duration of an activity more reliably if I sought expert advice?

Q Have I looked at previous project plans to see how long similar activities took?

Q Could I ask other project managers for their advice?

Q Am I confident that my estimates are realistic?

45 Get expert help to draw the first network diagram.

WORKING WITH A NETWORK DIAGRAM

A network diagram shows the relationship between activities, and which ones depend on the completion of others. The diagram may be simple or highly complex, according to how many activities there are and how they inter-relate. Where there are several routes through a network, there is a chance to complete tasks simultaneously. Indicate the duration of each task and add up the total time required to complete each route to find the longest route through the network. This longest route is known as the critical path, which shows the shortest possible duration for the project.

Key

Critical path (minimum duration 19 days)

Non-critical path (minimum duration 6 days)

Activities that can be undertaken simultaneously

Activity that can only start once previous activities are complete

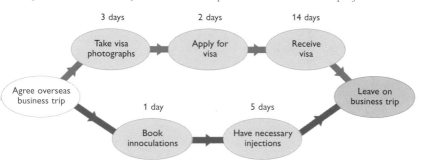

LOOKING FOR SLACK

You can also use the the network diagram to find opportunities for shortening the project schedule. This involves looking at where you can cut the amount of time it takes to complete activities on the critical path, for example, by increasing the resources available to that activity. Take another look at the diagram to identify where any other routes might have some slack. You may then be able to reallocate resources to reduce the pressure on the team members who are responsible for activities on the critical path.

▲ CREATING A NETWORK DIAGRAM

The network above sets out activities to be completed before a business trip. Progress on the critical path must be monitored closely, since a delay in carrying out these activities will affect the project end date.

46 Keep to the critical path to stay on schedule.

AGREEING DATES

Having identified how the activities follow on from one another, and worked out the minimum duration of the project, you can now set real dates. Plot these carefully, taking any potential conflicts into account, and then agree them with the team.

47 Start non-critical tasks as early as possible to free up resources later.

48 Remember to keep your Gantt chart up to date at all times.

USING A GANTT CHART ▼

This Gantt chart lists tasks on the left and the project time-scale in weeks across the top. The bars show when tasks start and finish, providing a clear visual overview of project tasks and timings.

CALCULATING DATES

Use the network diagram to help you calculate start and end dates for each activity. Begin with the first activity and work through all the others, starting each as early as possible to allow as much time as you can. If an activity is not on the critical path, start and end dates can be more flexible, since these will not necessarily affect the overall project duration. Finally, plot the dates against a timeline to produce a Gantt chart. These charts are useful for early schedule planning, for showing individual time-scales on complex projects, and for comparing progress to the original schedule.

Time-scale shows length of project

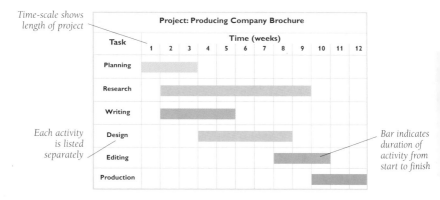

Each activity is listed separately

Bar indicates duration of activity from start to finish

LOOKING FOR OVERLAP

To check that the dates you have calculated are realistic, refer to your Gantt chart, commitment matrix, and master schedule. The Gantt chart shows you immediately where project activities overlap. Where an overlap exists, the commitment matrix will reveal whether an activity requires the same resource at the same time. In these circumstances, you will have to amend that activity's start and finish dates. The final piece of information comes from looking at the master schedule, which will tell you whether there is any overlap in resources between two projects or more.

49 Encourage your team members to be realistic about dates.

GAINING AGREEMENT

Discuss the dates you have set with the key people to make sure that they are truly available at the time they are needed. You may have to hold discussions with their managers if they are being held to other commitments elsewhere in the organization. On long projects, remember to allow for the fact that team members will not necessarily be available every day, even if they are theoretically working full-time on the project. The percentage of time they will be available is often around two-thirds of the calendar year, or 240 days. Use that number to check that you have allowed time off for holidays, sickness, and training.

◀ **PLANNING HOLIDAYS**
Ask team members to book in their holiday time as early as possible in order to avoid last-minute alterations to the schedule. Use a wallchart to show the team's holiday commitments.

35

VALIDATING THE PLAN

No matter how well you have written your plan, the unexpected is bound to occur and circumstances are certain to change. It is vital to work closely with the team and stakeholders to anticipate and pre-empt potential problems.

50 Make a point of discussing the final plan with your customers.

51 Use other project managers' experience to identify threats.

IDENTIFYING THREATS

Now that you have a schedule for all the activities needed to complete the project, brainstorm a list of potential threats and analyze each for its impact on your plan. People outside the team can be very helpful in this process, which also encourages the team to defend the plan against constructive criticism, making them more determined to overcome any obstacles. Deal with every threat in turn, paying most attention to those that have an impact on activities on the critical path so that you can work out your best counter-attack in advance.

ANTICIPATING ▼ PROBLEMS

Bring together a representative group of stakeholders, particularly customers, and those with relevant experience, and ask what could, in their opinion, go wrong.

Customer identifies potential problem

Sponsor weighs up impact on project

Project manager suggests a way of overcoming threat

Team member notes threats and suggested counter-attacks

PRE-EMPTING PROBLEMS

Now get the team to focus on preventing the problems from occurring. The question is, "What can we do to reduce the probability that each potential problem might occur?" If the plan is dependent on the weather, for example, you may change the timing of the work schedule. If key materials are in short supply or there is the possibility of industrial action in your own organization or that of your supplier, you must consider ways to address these problems early on.

52 If you suspect that someone may be promoted off the team, take steps to train a replacement.

53 Check contingency plans with whoever supplies resources.

54 Table the plan, with contingencies, at a review meeting.

CONTINGENCY PLANNING

It is not possible to pre-empt every eventuality that could harm the project. Get the team to consider what it will do if certain threats occur, and how to minimize the impact of the threats. If the project needs a new piece of software, for example, look at what you could do if it were to be delivered late. If the software is late, and you need a contingency system, it will probably add to the cost of the project. Bring this to the attention of those in control of budgets. You may then have to revisit your cost-benefit analysis.

COMPLETING THE PLAN

From the list of threats and the discussion on pre-empting problems and contingency planning, you will be able to decide what changes to make to the plan. Make these alterations and the plan is complete. The team has its "baseline" or starting point. It knows what the situation is now, and what will be the result of implementing the plan. Remember, though, that you must ensure that the team is prepared for the fact that the planning and implementation process is rarely sequential. It likely they will have to recast some of the plan as activities are carried out and changes occur.

POINTS TO REMEMBER

● The more stakeholders who validate a plan, the more likely it is to be implemented.

● If there is a strong likelihood that a contingency plan will be needed, that course of action should become the actual plan.

● Time spent validating the plan and preparing for problems in advance is rarely wasted.

● The entire plan should be double-checked by the project manager before implementation.

IMPLEMENTING A PLAN

The success of a project plan relies on the people who execute it. Equip yourself with the leadership skills necessary to build a strong, committed team and guide it to the desired outcome.

EXAMINING YOUR ROLE

To successfully implement a project plan, it is important to understand what is involved at the outset. Familiarize yourself with the key tasks, responsibilities, and skills involved, and you will be better prepared to lead a project team successfully.

> **55** Know the project plan inside out and answer questions authoritatively.

> **56** Keep the business priorities in mind, especially when the project goal is to make a profit.

DEFINING YOUR RESPONSIBILITIES

As project manager, you have overall responsibility for the project's success. Having negotiated the planning process, you must now translate the plan into action. This involves selecting the right team members, focusing and motivating them to achieve project goals, and helping them to develop both as individuals and as team workers. The project manager must also build good relationships with stakeholders, run team meetings effectively, administrate and co-ordinate, and communicate clearly on all levels every step of the way.

TAKING THE LEAD

A successful project manager is both a manager and leader. Leaders command authority and respect, follow up plans with actions, and are able to inspire and motivate others. They also adopt different leadership styles as circumstances dictate. You can develop these skills through training and experience: try practising outside work by taking office at your local sports club. Mainly, you develop leadership skills by taking responsibility for objectives. You may have to start by becoming accountable for a group of activities before you can take on an entire project.

Select final team members and allocate responsibilities

↓

Launch the project successfully

↓

Motivate and focus team on objectives

↓

Organize information systems

↓

Communicate key information

◀ **EVALUATING SKILLS**
To be an effective leader, you must develop several important attributes. This example shows some of the essential qualities of a successful project manager.

Is a good communicator

Can manage and adapt to change

Possesses the necessary technical expertise

Puts the customer first

Has team building and negotiating skills

QUESTIONS TO ASK YOURSELF

Q Are you willing to stay with the project for its entire term?

Q Are you interested in developing people and helping them to become leaders?

Q Do you have a real interest in working on the project?

Q Can you delegate objectives to the team as well as tasks?

ASSESSING YOURSELF

If you are not sure whether you have what it takes to be a leader, ask someone whose opinion you respect for objective comments. For example, you could talk to people with whom you have worked in the past to ascertain how they regard you. If they plainly feel that they could work for you, then that is a good indicator. Once you have gathered the facts, you can create a picture of where you want to be in the future, and put together a plan for developing the necessary skills.

BUILDING A TEAM

Having planned the project with a core team, now ensure that you have the full complement of people with the right mix of skills and personalities to see it through. Choose your team carefully, bearing in mind the vital team roles that should be covered.

57 Try not to have preconceived ideas about people – judge as you find.

QUESTIONS TO ASK YOURSELF

Q How much do I know about a potential team member and do I trust him or her?

Q Will I be able to work comfortably with him or her?

Q Am I confident that all the team members will get along with one another?

Q Does the team member have the necessary skills and talent to do the job – or will training be required?

ASSESSING AVAILABILITY

Refer back to your commitment matrix to identify the skills and people needed to complete the project. The chart will tell you who is required, for how long, and when. Draw up a list of candidates who might be suitable for each part and find out whether they are available. You may need to negotiate with other managers if you wish to appoint staff working in different areas of the organization. Your own project is almost certainly not the only one in progress, so you may also need to talk to whoever is co-ordinating the resources deployed on all of the projects.

CHOOSING THE RIGHT PEOPLE

Apart from having the necessary skills, the people you want to attract are those who will come willingly. It is much easier to work with people who are enthusiastic about the project, so it pays to hold discussions with potential team members to find out whether they are keen to work on the project. Think also of the team as a whole. Will each team member fit in with the others? Is there any conflict between potential members? You will, of course, help them to form a team under your leadership, but it is better to start off with people who are sympathetic to each other.

58 Be frank with potential team members – ask if they identify with the project's aims.

59 Build a team that takes advantage of each individual's skills without overburdening their weaknesses.

CONSIDERING ROLES

In any team you will look for people to carry out a team role as well as their functional role. To operate efficiently you, as the team leader, will want someone to perform the roles of critic, implementer, external contact, co-ordinator, ideas person, team builder, and inspector. Most team members will fit strongly into one or more of these roles. You need them all, and if one is not present, you will have to take the role on yourself. If, for example, you see that no one is challenging the team's standards, quality, and way of working, you are lacking a critic. Keep challenging the team yourself until you see someone else leaning towards this role. Discuss these roles in an open manner, encourage friendly conversations, and you will build one of the most important qualities of a group – team spirit. Remember that only as a team will you be able to achieve the project's objectives.

KEY TEAM ROLES

CO-ORDINATOR
Pulls together the work of the team as a whole.

CRITIC
Guardian and analyst of the team's effectiveness.

IDEAS PERSON
Encourages the team's innovative vitality.

IMPLEMENTER
Ensures smooth-running of the team's actions.

EXTERNAL CONTACT
Looks after the team's external contacts.

INSPECTOR
Ensures high standards are maintained.

TEAM BUILDER
Develops the teamworking spirit.

DO'S AND DON'TS

✔ Do allow people to settle into roles without being pushed.

✔ Do double or treble up on roles when a project team only has a few members.

✔ Do ask a stakeholder to take on a role if it is not being played.

✘ Don't attempt to shoehorn a personality into a particular role.

✘ Don't expect people to continue playing a role if they become uncomfortable in it.

✘ Don't take on a role yourself if it means appearing insincere.

60 Encourage criticism, but ask the critic to supply alternatives, too.

STARTING POSITIVELY

*O*nce you have the right team in place, it is important to launch a new project in a positive manner. Encourage teamwork by inviting everyone to an informal gathering at the outset, and record the project's existence formally to clarify its purpose.

61 Ask the most senior person possible to attend a project launch.

62 Listen to reactions from newcomers and be prepared to review activities.

USING YOUR SPONSOR ▼
The first team meeting offers your sponsor an important platform. Invite him or her to address the team and express belief and commitment in the project. This is invaluable for encouraging team spirit.

STARTING ACTIVELY

At an early stage, gather the team together for a full initiation session to let them know exactly what the project is all about. Explain what the targets and constraints are, let everyone know how the project will benefit them, and establish ground rules relating to the sharing of information and decision-making. Keep the session two-way so that people can ask questions. By the end of the meeting, everyone should understand what needs to be done, and feel motivated to achieve it.

Colleague feels valued in his new role

Sponsor greets team with positive enthusiasm

Team member learns of the project's importance

Team member is impressed by sponsor's confidence in the project manager and team

WRITING A START-UP REPORT

A start-up report should make everyone aware of the vision that has inspired the project and the measures of success the team will be aiming for. You may also document the resources allocated to the project, and give some indication of the risks that are involved. Finally, it is a good idea to name all the stakeholders so that everyone knows who they are, and ask key people who are underpinning the project to endorse it by adding their signatures to the document. These will include the project manager and project sponsor.

63 Keep reports free of jargon and complex language.

64 Ask for signatures to the plan as a formal agreement.

STRUCTURING A START-UP REPORT

PARTS OF A REPORT	FACTORS TO INCLUDE
VISION An explanation of the overall aim of the project.	● Clarify exactly why the project has been initiated and what it is setting out to achieve. ● Spell out the benefits of the project to the entire project team and to the organization as a whole.
TARGETS A summary of indicators, current performance, and target figures.	● Provide clear information on how the success of the project will be measured. ● Explain what business results are expected to have been achieved by the end of the project.
MILESTONES Special events or achievements that mark progress along the way.	● Summarize milestones to remind everyone of what they will have to deliver at each stage of the project ● Set out your milestones so that they divide the project into logical, measurable segments.
RISKS AND OPPORTUNITIES A list of the potential risks and additional opportunities.	● Explain what needs to be avoided when team members carry out their roles. ● Highlight any areas where improvements could be made in order to gain even greater benefit from the project.
LIST OF STAKEHOLDERS A directory of all the stakeholders involved in the project.	● Name all interested parties and list their credentials to add to the credibility of the project. ● List all your customers, and state what each customer expects to gain from the project.

LEADING EFFECTIVELY

There are many different styles of leadership, but because projects rely on good teamwork, it is important to favour a consensus-building, rather than a dictatorial, approach. To lead a project well, you must be able to motivate your team.

65 Be a manager whom people want to seek out, rather than avoid.

66 Show your enthusiasm for the project, even when under pressure.

UNDERSTANDING STYLES

There is a spectrum of possibilities in leadership styles, and you will need to adopt them all at certain points in the project. While your approach may need to vary from a dictatorial style to a consensus-seeking one, the predominant style you adopt should depend on your organization, the nature of the project, the characteristics of the team, and your own personality.

CHOOSING A LEADERSHIP STYLE

LEADERSHIP STYLE	WHEN TO USE IT
DICTATORIAL Making decisions alone, taking risks, being autocratic and controlling.	This style may be appropriate if the project faces a crisis, and there is no time to consult. However, since it discourages teamwork, it should be used sparingly.
ANALYTICAL Gathering all the facts, observing and analyzing before reaching decisions.	This style, which requires sound analytical skills, may be used when a project is under time pressure or threat, and the right decision must be made quickly.
OPINION-SEEKING Asking for opinions from the team on which to base decisions.	Use this style to build team confidence and show that you value people's views, as well as to impress stakeholders, who like to be consulted.
DEMOCRATIC Encouraging team participation and involvement in decision-making.	This is an essential style to be used on a regular basis to empower team members, and help strengthen their commitment to a project.

CULTURAL DIFFERENCES

Project managers in the UK often create an inner circle of key team members to speed up decision-making, while in the US, the entire team is brought together frequently. In Japan, decisions are reached by consensus, in which unanimous agreement is reached through a laborious process.

CHANGING STYLES

Be prepared to change your leadership style to suit the circumstances and the team, even if you feel uncomfortable for a while because the style you are adopting does not come naturally. For example, some managers find consultation annoying and time-wasting, while other managers are so intent on gaining consensus that decisions take too long, and the project suffers as a result. The key to making good consensus decisions is to listen carefully to everyone before indicating which way they are leaning. A decision is then reached accordingly, unless someone can argue most convincingly that it is the wrong move.

LEADING APPROPRIATELY

Each member of a team has a unique personality and style. Take time to study each individual and understand what motivates them so that you can provide the level of guidance they need. Some team members will prefer to be set objectives, with the project manager delegating responsibility to them for how they should be tackled. Others will react better to being given specific tasks. Use the appropriate style for each individual.

▼ **ADOPTING A HANDS-OFF APPROACH**
Motivate an experienced, capable team member by allowing them to use their own initiative. Provide support and guidance but avoid interfering too heavily.

◀ **BEING HANDS-ON**
Explain clearly what you expect from a new or less confident worker, who will need close supervision and encouragement.

45

Obtaining Results

There are two major factors to consider when deciding which style of leadership to use. If the project is under time pressure, there may be no alternative to the dictatorial style because you do not have the luxury of time to consult. If you want to gain commitment, you must involve others in the key decisions to increase their willingness to make the decision work. Whichever style you choose, the quality of the decision is vital. Before you impose a decision, ensure that you have all the facts to prove that it is the right thing to do.

67 Look for ways to use conflict constructively.

Resolving Conflict

Personality clashes are inevitable when many people work together. There may be differences of opinion or disputes that arise from people having different standards on quality of work, or there may be one or two team members who simply do not get on. If team members are in disagreement find a way of resolving the conflict either by taking on the role of decision-maker yourself or by using diplomacy in talking to the people concerned.

Conflicts can sometimes arise as a result of schedules. For example one team member might want more time for a group of activities, which a colleague feels is unnecessary. Work through the schedule with both parties to arrive at a solution that suits everyone.

◀ BEING A DIPLOMAT
When a conflict between team members threatens the project's success, you will have to mediate. Look for a solution that brings some source of satisfaction to each party. Such a compromise will allow the project to move on.

CASE STUDY

...ly, a key member of the ...oject team, was responsible ...r leading a small team of her ...wn. As the project got under ...way, Tom, the project manager, ...was surprised to see that Gerald, one of Sally's most competent and confident team members, was contributing very little to team meetings. He took Gerald aside informally and asked how he was getting on. Although Tom was reluctant to criticize Sally,

by listening carefully, Tom realized that Gerald had been used to far more involvement in making decisions on other project teams he had worked for. It was evident that Gerald found Sally too abrupt. Tom approached Sally and asked her to think about her leadership style with Gerald. As a result, she spent more time discussing issues with him, and Gerald went on to play a far more active part in team meetings once again.

◀ **LEADING WISELY**

Sally's abrupt approach and her tendency to make all the decisions was very demotivating for Gerald, who liked to be able to use his initiative. Rather than take matters into his own hands, Tom asked Sally to consider the matter and take any action she deemed appropriate. Sally decided to make a point of involving Gerald more to make him feel valued. As a result, his performance soon began to improve.

...TANDING BACK

...can be a hard lesson to learn that a good leader ...ill allow people to make a mistake. You may, ...om your experience, know that the team is ...king a decision that is not in the best interests of ...e project. But if you take control, you are not ...ecessarily helping them to improve. If they never ...e the effects of their decisions, they will never ...arn which ones led to difficulties. Obviously, you ...ust use your discretion as to when to step back. ...he team's development is important, but not as ...tal as achieving the objectives of the project.

68 Show your team respect, and they will show it to you.

69 Introduce new ideas to maintain the team's interest.

EXERCISING LEADERSHIP SKILLS

To lead your team effectively, you must:
- Ensure that everyone is working towards agreed, shared objectives;
- Criticize constructively, and praise good work as well as find fault;
- Monitor team members' activities continuously by obtaining effective feedback, such as regular reports;

- Constantly encourage and organize the generation of new ideas within the team, using techniques such as brainstorming;
- Always insist on the highest standards of execution from team members;
- Develop the individual and collective skills of the team, and seek to strengthen them by training and recruitment.

DEVELOPING TEAMWORK

*F*or a team to be successful, people must learn to pull together. Encourage teamwork by promoting a positive atmosphere in which people compete with ideas rather than egos, and recognize the team's changing needs as it progresses through the project.

70 When individuals perform well, praise them in front of the team.

CULTURAL DIFFERENCES

Project managers in the US often use rousing speeches and rhetoric to motivate staff and build team spirit. In the UK, an eloquent speech will also strengthen commitment, but the approach has to be far more subtle. In Japan, managers seek to build strong ties of loyalty by emphasizing the importance of the project to the company.

ENCOURAGING TEAMWORK

Make sure that each member of the team recognizes the value that everyone else is bringing to the project. Encourage them to appreciate one another's skills and capabilities, and to work together to achieve the highest standards. Praise the team as well as individuals so that everyone feels that they are doing a good job. If everyone understands who is playing which role and who has responsibility for what, there should be no reason for conflict and uncertainty. As project manager, you must be seen to be fair to everyone since showing any favouritism can also lead to dissent. Use project review meetings to strengthen teamwork and help build team confidence.

UNDERSTANDING TEAM DEVELOPMENT

All teams go through a series of stages as they develop, described as forming, storming, norming, and performing. Your aim is to move the team on to the performing stage, where they are working well together, as quickly as possible. With strong leadership, the difficult initial stages of bringing the team together and settling them into the project can be negotiated smoothly. Use your authority to swiftly defuse any conflict and put a stop to any early political manoeuvring.

POINTS TO REMEMBER

● Not every team member will be equally committed to the project at the outset.

● It should be expected that everyone will have to go through the storming stage, but this can be creative if managed positively.

● It is important to develop creative team members rather than conformists.

● People need to be comfortable to work well together.

DEALING WITH STAGES IN THE LIFE OF A PROJECT TEAM

FORMING
Members feel tentative and unsure about their project roles

Explain what everyone will contribute

STORMING
Members try to assert their positions and jockey for seniority

Make it clear that teamwork is crucial to success

Foster team spirit and develop the team's skills

NORMING
Working practices and processes are agreed and established

Build team confidence in its collective ability

PERFORMING
Team works positively and productively to achieve project goals

Keep the team focused on completing project

MAINTAINING MOMENTUM

There are two more stages that occur in a team's long-term life, known as "boring" and "mourning". The first applies to a project lasting a long time, where team members may stop looking for new challenges or new and improved ways of doing things. Put in effort at this stage to encourage innovation. Mourning occurs when a team has bonded well and reacts to a member's departure by grieving their loss. Decide how to replace that person and reassure remaining team members that you have every confidence in their ability.

71 Help people to define problems for themselves.

72 Remember that relationships will change over time.

MAKING TEAM DECISIONS

When mapping out the future course of the project, quality decision-making is paramount. To ensure that you make the right decisions as a team, establish a logical process that you follow every time. Then use feedback to double-check quality.

73 Ensure that you know all the facts before making a decision.

USING A LOGICAL PROCESS

Following the same process in making every decision has several benefits. The team becomes faster at decision-making, since if everyone knows the process, they quickly eliminate invalid options and come to the most sensible alternative. The quality of decisions improves because using a process removes some of the guesswork and, finally, any team members who might initially have been against a decision are more likely to accept it if it has been reached via a process of consensus.

DEFINING THE IDEAL

The team must agree on the criteria against which they wish to measure a decision and the ideal performance against each criterion. Suppose, for example, you are looking at two options for a supplier of services to the project. Ask team members to brainstorm what an ideal solution would look like. Ask the questions, "What do we want this solution to do for us?", and "What benefits should we look for?" This list then gives the team a way of filtering options and comparing the alternatives.

▼ AGREEING CRITERIA
Brainstorm a list of criteria against which you will measure decisions, and ask a team member to record each suggestion on a flipchart so that everyone is using the same wording to describe the ideal.

EVALUATING OPTIONS

With the team's help, identify which criteria are the most important. You may find that three or four stand out as being vital. Now measure all your options against the ideal agreed for each criterion. The process is logical, but good creative thinking is still needed to evaluate the options effectively. Having carried out this evaluation, you may find that the decision is obvious. If not, take the next most important criterion and repeat the exercise. Continue until one option stands out, or until the team is certain that, say, two options have nothing between them. Where that is the case, choose the option you believe will be the most acceptable to your sponsor and other stakeholders.

74 Encourage debate on all the options to gain a wider perspective.

75 Ask an objective critic to look at your decision and give you feedback.

MAKING SAFE DECISIONS

What would be the impact if you made a wrong decision? If it would be catastrophic, you may want to think again and find a less risky route. Finally use the acronym SAFE to validate the choice. SAFE stands for:

● Suitable: is the decision really the most suitable one, given the current state of the project?

● Acceptable: is the decision acceptable to all the stakeholders who have an interest in it?

● Feasible: will it be practical and feasible to implement the solution, given the project's time and resource constraints?

● Enduring: will the solution endure to the end of the project and further into the long term?

Remember that the SAFE test can be applied as a quick and useful check for any decision made by teams or individuals.

VALIDATING DECISIONS ▶
Check that you have made the right decisions by asking your sponsor or other stakeholders, such as customers or suppliers, for their views.

MANAGING INFORMATION

Everyone must have easy access to key project information whenever they need it. You can ensure that all the project data is kept up to date and recorded efficiently by setting up a knowledge centre and appointing a co-ordinator to manage it.

76 Keep notes of errors made and lessons learned for future reference.

77 Index information clearly to make it more accessible.

78 Check that data is being updated on a regular basis.

ASSESSING INFORMATION

During the life of a project you will produce a wealth of data. Each item of information should be regarded as potentially valuable, either to your own project or to a subsequent one. It will be obvious what must be stored, but try to think more widely. If, for example, a project involves researching a benchmark for productivity, remember that this may be of interest to other parts of the organization. Any work undertaken on risk management, new techniques used, or even the way in which the team has been structured could prove valuable in the future.

ORGANIZING DATA

Project data can be grouped into two types: general planning information, such as the vision statement, objectives, master schedule, and network diagram; and general data, such as any background information that might be needed to carry out activities. It may be a good idea to divide activity information into three further groups: completed activities; activities currently in progress; and activities still to be started. In this way, everyone will know exactly where to look for the information they need. Beware of amassing lots of unnecessary data, however, because this will simply clog up what should be an efficient, easy-to-use system.

THINGS TO DO

1. Explain to the team what type of information is to go into the knowledge centre.
2. Ensure that the knowledge co-ordinator has the necessary software tools to run the centre efficiently.
3. Ask the co-ordinator to remind people of deadlines for completing activities and progress reports.

APPOINTING A CO-ORDINATOR

In projects where the information flow is limited, you will probably be able to manage the data yourself. However, in a large project with a mass of information, it will pay dividends to put a team member in charge of the knowledge centre, either full-time or part-time. Such a person is known as the knowledge co-ordinator, and the most likely candidate for the job is the team member who most takes on the role of co-ordinator. He or she will keep the planning documentation up to date and collect, index, and make available all the important project information gathered by the team.

CULTURAL DIFFERENCES

Business organizations in North America tend to lead the way when it comes to saving information and making it available to the organization as a whole. Most organizations in the US employ knowledge co-ordinators at several levels, meaning that project managers are able to access information quickly and easily. Knowledge co-ordinators are gradually making their presence felt in Europe as their importance becomes recognized.

◀ **UPDATING PROJECT INFORMATION**
The knowledge co-ordinator plays an important role as the administrator of the project plan, collecting progress reports, updating network diagrams, Gantt charts, and activity reports.

Team member updates co-ordinator on progress of an activity

Co-ordinator records information for knowledge centre

COMMUNICATING CLEARLY

The better the communication, the more smoothly a project will flow. Make sure that everyone who needs it has easy access to project information, and that you encourage two-way communication by listening and asking for feedback.

79 Avoid sending any message that could hinder, rather than help, your project.

80 Tell the team what they want and need to know.

81 Meet often with team members on a one-to-one basis.

SHARING KNOWLEDGE

Consider who needs what information, in what format, and when. Refer to the list of stakeholder in the start-up report to ensure that no-one is forgotten. Concentrate on people whose access to information will be crucial to the project, but do not ignore others with less significant roles. Plan how you are going to make the information available, bearing in mind that these activities should take up as little time as possible. Your knowledge co-ordinator must know what the priorities are. For example, if a customer changes requirements, the team needs to know urgently.

USING INFORMATION TECHNOLOGY

Make the most of new technology to improve communications. E-mail is an extremely useful time-saving device, provided it is handled correctly. The main point to remember is that you receive as many e-mails as you send, which means that you should think carefully before writing each message. Is it absolutely vital to send a message now? Is it the most effective means of communication for the current situation? As a guideline, send as few e-mails as possible to do the job well, and you will get the best out of electronic communication. Take care too, with compatibility. E-mailing an electronic file to someone who does not have the same software results in an immediate communication breakdown. This wastes time.

ENCOURAGING TWO-WAY COMMUNICATION

The team is the primary conduit for information between the customer, other stakeholders, and you, the project manager. It is important to encourage honest feedback. Use open questions, such as the ones below, to ascertain their real feelings and opinions.

❝ *How do you think we could improve the way we are working on this project?* ❞

❝ *How are our customers reacting to the work we are doing – do they appear to be satisfied?* ❞

❝ *Having completed that activity, is there anything you would change if you had to do it again?* ❞

❝ *Are you aware of any negative reactions concerning the progress of the project?* ❞

LISTENING TO OTHERS

Encourage the project team to be open and honest with you by showing that you value their opinions and are willing to listen to them. Make it clear that even negative feedback is viewed as a positive opportunity for improvement, and ensure that team members are not intimidated by fear of any repercussions when they do express criticisms. Keep your door open for stakeholders, too – it is important that they feel they can approach you with queries or problems. Always listen to people carefully – because only through listening can you determine whether your messages have really been understood.

82 Be interested both in what people say and how they are saying it.

Team member feels free to voice an honest opinion

Colleague provides both negative and positive feedback

◀ INVITING FEEDBACK

Take team members aside, either individually or in small groups, and solicit feedback by asking for their comments on how they think the project is progressing.

MONITORING PERFORMANCE

Effective monitoring keeps a project on track in terms of performance, time, and cost. Focus on your plan while acting fast to tackle problems and changes in order to stay on course.

TRACKING PROGRESS

Even the best-laid plans can go awry, which is why it is crucial to have an early-warning monitoring system. Make sure that you understand what effective monitoring involves and how to set up a process that will highlight potential problems.

83 Keep comparing current schedules and budgets against the original plan.

84 Never relax control, even when all is going to plan.

85 Ask the team for ideas on speeding up progress.

MONITORING EFFECTIVELY

Keeping control of a project involves carefully managing your plan to keep it moving forward smoothly. Effective monitoring allows you to gather information so that you can measure and adjust progress towards the project's goals. It enables you to communicate project progress and changes to team members, stakeholders, superiors, and customers, and gives you the justification for making any necessary adjustmen to the plan. It also enables you to measure curren progress against that set out in the original plan.

MONITORING SUPPLIERS

External suppliers can be a threat, since you do not have direct control over their resources. Remember to ensure that you monitor their progress, too. Make them feel part of the team by inviting them to meetings and informal gatherings. This will help you to track their progress throughout their involvement in the project, rather than only when they are due to deliver.

USING REPORTS

Anyone responsible for an activity or a milestone must report on progress. Encourage the team to take reports seriously, and to submit them on time. Reports should record the current state of the project, achievements since the last report, and potential problems, opportunities, or threats to milestones. As project manager, you review the reports and summarize the current position for your sponsor and stakeholders. Having gauged the importance of issues reported, use a red, amber, and green status system to help you draw up your review meeting agenda, so that the most urgent items, or those with red status, take priority.

POINTS TO REMEMBER

- If the project is a large or complex one, reports will be required more frequently.

- When a project involves tackling issues for the first time, tight and frequent controls should be established.

- If team members are used to working on their own, too frequent monitoring may be counter-productive.

UNDERSTANDING THE MONITORING PROCESS

Team members prepare progress reports

↓

Project manager summarizes for sponsor and stakeholders

↓

Items for discussion are listed on regular review meeting agenda

↓

Regular review meeting is held to resolve issues and assess progress

↓

Periodic meetings are held to monitor milestones

↓

Plans are updated if necessary to keep project on track

CONSIDERING TIMING

Think about how often you will need progress reports and review meetings. You may require weekly or even daily reports, depending on the potential harm a problem could do to the project were it not detected and reported. Regular review meetings provide an opportunity to resolve issues, discuss progress and review performance. You should hold reviews at least once a month, and probably more often on a complex project, or one going through a particularly demanding phase.

HOLDING REVIEW MEETINGS

Review meetings are held throughout the life of a project to discuss progress and achievements and mark milestones. Run these meetings effectively to encourage teamwork and provide all involved with an accurate picture of how the project is faring.

86 Encourage team members to speak out on any aspect of the project.

87 Ensure that review meetings are not tediously long.

88 If progress has been made, praise people's efforts.

PLANNING A REVIEW

There are two types of review meeting. A regular formal review occurs at least monthly to monitor detailed achievements and issues in implementing the plan. An event-driven review, to which stakeholders, such as your sponsor, will be invited is held as certain milestones are arrived at. These meetings are concerned with the business objectives of the project. They may be called to check that the project is meeting certain criteria. It is sometimes true that if the criteria are not met, the future of the project will be in doubt.

SELECTING ATTENDEES

You will need your sponsor at some meetings, but probably not all. Key team members will almost certainly attend all reviews, while other members should attend only if there is a valid reason for their attendance, or their time will be wasted. If someone need only be present for one or two items, estimate when you will reach those items and ask them to arrive a few minutes earlier. If you need to make a decision, ensure that the person with the authority to make the decision is present and that all the necessary information is available.

QUESTIONS TO ASK YOURSELF

Q Will every attendee have a valid contribution to make?

Q Are there some team members who only need to attend part of the meeting?

Q Is this team member attending the meeting because they have always done so, rather than for a specific purpose?

Q Does the absence of anyone pose a threat to the project?

Use progress report to compile agenda	→	Decide who needs to attend review	→	Circulate agenda to participants

CHAIRING A REVIEW

The key to chairing a review meeting successfully is good discipline. Summarize the objectives at the outset and allocate time to each item on the agenda. Focus the team on appraisal rather than analysis, using questions such as, "How is the project going?" and "What new issues have arisen since the last meeting?" Your aim is to keep everyone up to date with progress and give them a shared understanding of what is happening.

▲ PREPARING FOR MEETINGS

Key decisions are made at review meetings, so it is essential to prepare for them well. Send out agendas in advance to give the team time to do preparation work, too.

Team member arrives late for meeting

Project manager sets standards for punctuality in future

ESTABLISHING ▶ DISCIPLINE
Be prepared to be tough on latecomers. Make it clear from the outset that such behaviour is unacceptable, stressing the fact that one person's lateness wastes everyone's time.

89 Remind people of the agenda when they stray from it.

90 Always seek to end a meeting on a positive note.

REINFORCING OBJECTIVES

Ensure that you return to the objectives throughout the meeting, recording which have been achieved, which remain, and how the meeting is going against the time plan. If people are straying from the point or talking irrelevantly, bring the discussion back to the main issue by saying, for example, "We are not here to discuss that today – let's get back to the point." At appropriate moments, summarize the views and decisions made. As objectives are achieved, consider releasing those people who are no longer needed.

OVERCOMING PROBLEMS

However sound the project plan, once you start to operate in the real world, problems will occur. Encourage team members to raise concerns, and use the discipne of problem-solving techniques to tackle difficulties as they arise.

91 Look at every aspect of a problem before trying to resolve it.

92 Remember that forewarned is forearmed.

93 Ask team members to bring you solutions as well as problems.

RAISING CONCERNS

Your primary aim is to identify problems early enough to prevent their becoming crises. It is far more difficult to take action when a problem has become urgent. Although you may create extra work by examining problems that do not ultimately occur, it is better to err on the side of caution than to find that a problem has escalated without your knowledge. With experience, the team will get better at judging whether and when to raise a concern. You should be particularly concerned to see that problems with a high impact on the project are spotted and action taken before they become high urgency as well.

CASE STUDY

John was put in charge of a new project to improve the inventory control system in his organization's main warehouse. However, once the project was under way, he was approached by Tom, the warehouse manager, who told John that he and his warehouse staff were having to spend an inordinate amount of time chasing up deliveries deemed to be late by a member of the project team. Tom explained that most of the queries raised by the team member were unnecessary, because the goods were generally delivered only a few hours late, and so asking warehouse staff to chase them seemed pointless. John called Tom and the project team together to agree when a query really needed to be raised. This reduced the strain on warehouse staff, and gave everyone more time to chase up deliveries that really were late.

◀ **HANDLING TENSIONS**
Since projects tend to be carried out alongside regular business operations, problems often result when the two are ongoing. In this case, the project members were trying to make improvements by identifying late deliveries. But by raising concerns too early, they were disrupting the usual warehouse work. By agreeing when to raise concerns, both teams were able to do their jobs more effectively.

DEALING WITH PROBLEMS

Listen to concerns raised by team members

Discuss their impact and, if significant, look at the options with the team

Take an overview and make a final decision

Update the plan if the decision involves altering course

Send updated plan to knowledge co-ordinator

RESOLVING DIFFICULTIES

A useful problem-solving technique is to home in on four areas to find out which is causing difficulty. For example, if production is falling short of target, consider which of the following four P's could be the culprit:

- **People** Is the problem occurring because people do not have the right skills or support?
- **Product** Is there something wrong in the design of the product or the production method?
- **Process** Would an improvement in one of your business processes cure the problem?
- **Procurement** Is it something to do with the products and services we buy?

DO'S AND DON'TS

✔ Do keep in constant touch with suppliers who may be causing you problems.

✔ Do correct a recurring problem by changing a process.

✗ Don't start to resolve an issue until you have understood the whole problem.

✗ Don't assume that team members have problem-solving skills

UPDATING THE PLAN

Ask your project co-ordinator to document on-going problem-solving activities in the knowledge centre as open items, and assess them at your regular review meetings. Major issues may result in the need to make significant changes to the plan. It is even possible that new information or a change in the external environment will invalidate the project as it stands. Suppose, for example, that a competitor brings out a new product using components that makes your project irrelevant. This would be unfortunate, but since your priority is to deliver value to your organization, the best value may lie in scrapping the project.

94 Keep stakeholders informed if you change the plan.

95 Identify the cause of a problem to prevent it from happening again.

DEALING WITH CHANGE

Change is inevitable on projects, so flexibility is vital. Whether customers revise a brief or senior managers alter the scope of a project, you must be able to negotiate changes, adapt the plan, and keep everyone informed about what is happening.

96 Look at alternatives before changing a major component of the plan.

97 Explain the benefits of change to those affected by it.

98 Seek approval for any changes as quickly as possible.

UNDERSTANDING CHANGE

Some changes will be within your control, such as shortening the schedule because you and your team are learning how to complete activities more quickly as you work through the plan. Other changes will be imposed upon you, such as when a customer asks for something different or a superior decides to poach two of your key team members to do another job. Alternatively, your monitoring system may have highlighted the need for a change to avoid a potential problem or threat. Whenever the need for change arises, it is vital to be able to adjust the project plan as necessary. You must also be able to measure whether the desired effect on the project has been achieved, so that you will know if the change has been successful.

◀ **DISCUSSING CHANGE**
Bring the team together to evaluate how changes might affect the project plan, looking at the proposed alterations against your original goals, order of activities, budget, people, resources, and time.

ASSESSING IMPACT

Before you commit to making any changes, assess their impact on the project. Ask the team to review how they will affect the schedule, budget, and resources. Examine the alternatives: is there another way to accomplish the project's objectives? If changes have to be made for the project to move forward, document them on the original plan, and gain approval from superiors, sponsors, and stakeholders before implementing them.

RESISTING UNNECESSARY OR DETRIMENTAL CHANGES

When change is dictated, perhaps by a superior or sponsor, it may not always make sense. Determine whether carrying out the change will affect the eventual outcome of the project. If the change seems to be frivolous, or will have a negative impact on the project, make those imposing it aware of the benefits that will be lost. Be prepared to fight your corner, or to offer alternative solutions that will ensure your project still meets its objectives.

TACKLING CHANGE EFFECTIVELY

Discuss impact of change with the team

If change has a major impact, look at the alternatives

Document necessary changes on original plan

Seek approval from stakeholders and superiors

Inform everyone on the project of changes as soon as possible

THINGS TO DO

1. Talk to the team about how changes will affect them.

2. Explain the rationale behind the changes and why they had to happen.

3. Redefine new objectives, time-scales, or roles.

4. Discuss issues individually if anyone is still unhappy about the changes.

COMMUNICATING CHANGE

If your team has been working hard to achieve one set of objectives and is suddenly told that the goal posts have changed, people will inevitably feel demotivated. Talk to the team about change as soon as possible, particularly if roles are affected. Focus on the positive aspects of change, and be frank about why it is happening. Take people's concerns seriously, listen to their ideas, but stress the need to adapt as quickly as possible. Finally, spell out clearly any new expectations, schedules, or objectives in writing, so that everyone understands what should happen next.

MAXIMIZING IMPACT

As a project draws to a close, it is important to evaluate exactly what has been achieved and what can be learned for the next time. Take your project through a formal close-down process that ties up all loose ends and marks its success.

99 Evaluate this project well to better manage the next one.

QUESTIONS TO ASK YOURSELF

Q Is the sponsor satisfied that the original aims and business objectives of the project have been met?

Q Is the customer satisfied that he or she is receiving an improved service?

Q Have we spoken to all our stakeholders about final results?

Q Have I thanked all the contributors to the project?

Q Have all new insights and ideas been recorded?

SEEING PROJECTS THROUGH

Inevitably towards the end of a project, some team members will start to move to new assignments. It is important to keep remaining team members focused on final objectives until the very end of the project, when you write a formal close-down report and hold a final meeting. You may have to protect your resources from being moved off the project too early, particularly if you want to avoid an untidy ending where the benefits are dissipated because final activities are completed haphazardly. Finally, you want your organization to learn as much as possible from the exercise and to ensure that the results you predicted are delivered in full.

LEARNING FROM PROJECTS

Talk to your knowledge co-ordinator about publishing a report explaining what the project achieved, and detailing relevant information such as facts gathered and processes used. If the project is likely to be repeated, meet with team members to go through the project from start to finish. Ask people to point out where, with hindsight, they could have made improvements. Your organization may benefit significantly if you produce a template for such a project plan, including an outline network and Gantt chart.

100 Ensure that you have not left any jobs unfinished.

101 Publicize the achievements of the project team.

Compiling a Close-Down Report

Parts of Report	Factors to Consider
Performance Indicators A comparison of what the project has achieved against the original targets set.	● Explain in full the reasons for any variances between targets and actual achievements. ● Word the comparison in a way that validates the original investment appraisal.
Resource Utilization An assessment of the resources planned and those that were actually used.	● If the project used more or fewer resources than expected, state the reasons why. ● Include any information that will validate the budget allocated to the project.
Strengths and Weaknesses An appraisal of what went well on the project and what went wrong, or caused problems.	● Ask team members for input in order to conduct as thorough an analysis as possible. ● Make sure that the information recorded enables others to learn from this experience.
Success Factors A record of the top 10 factors judged to be critical to the success of your project	● List your success factors with the help of the team, sponsor, and stakeholders. ● Create a list that will provide focus for future project managers.

▼ CELEBRATING SUCCESS
Mark the end of a project with a celebration in recognition of the team's hard work and effort. This allows people to say their farewells and realize their achievements in a convivial atmosphere.

Thanking the Team

It is important that all the members of the team go their separate ways feeling as positive as possible, especially since you may want to work with the same people on subsequent projects. Indeed, good relationships should be kept up with all the stakeholders. Talk to everyone individually to thank them for their contributions. Hold a final meeting at which your sponsor can confirm that the project has indeed brought benefits and thank the team for its efforts. Your customers, in particular, may welcome an opportunity to express how they have found the results of the project.

ASSESSING YOUR PROJECT MANAGEMENT SKILLS

Evaluate your ability to think strategically by responding to the following statements, marking the option closest to your experience. Be as honest as you can: if your answer is "never", circle Option 1; if it is "always", circle Option 4, and so on. Add your scores together, and refer to the Analysis to see how well you scored. Use your answers to identify the areas that most need improvement.

OPTIONS
1 Never
2 Occasionally
3 Frequently
4 Always

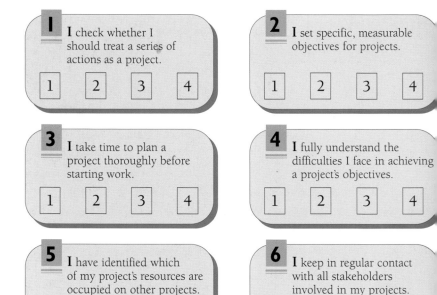

1 I check whether I should treat a series of actions as a project.

1   2   3   4

2 I set specific, measurable objectives for projects.

1   2   3   4

3 I take time to plan a project thoroughly before starting work.

1   2   3   4

4 I fully understand the difficulties I face in achieving a project's objectives.

1   2   3   4

5 I have identified which of my project's resources are occupied on other projects.

1   2   3   4

6 I keep in regular contact with all stakeholders involved in my projects.

1   2   3   4

7 I always consider what the ideal outcome of a project would be.

1 2 3 4

8 I ensure that everyone clearly understands the project's objectives.

1 2 3 4

9 I set business targets for each part of a project.

1 2 3 4

10 I check that a project will not unnecessarily change what already works.

1 2 3 4

11 I compile a full list of project activities before I place them in correct order.

1 2 3 4

12 I calculate manpower time and elapsed time of all project activities.

1 2 3 4

13 I make sure all the key people have approved the plan before I start a project.

1 2 3 4

14 I liaise with the finance department to check the costs of a project.

1 2 3 4

15 I generally start project implementation with a pilot.

1 2 3 4

16 I keep a network diagram up to date throughout a project.

1 2 3 4

17 I inform all interested parties of changes to project resource requirements.

1 2 3 4

18 I prepare contingency plans for all major risks to the project.

1 2 3 4

19 I adapt my leadership style to suit circumstances and individuals.

1 2 3 4

20 I consider how best to develop my teams' skills.

1 2 3 4

21 I consider how well new team members will fit in with the rest of the team.

1 2 3 4

22 I make sure each team member knows exactly what is expected of them.

1 2 3 4

23 I use my sponsor to help motivate my team.

1 2 3 4

24 I have documented and circulated the primary milestones of the project.

1 2 3 4

25 I ensure that every team member has access to the information they need.

1 2 3 4

26 I avoid keeping secrets from the project team and stakeholders.

1 2 3 4

27 I ask people to attend review meetings only if they really need to be present.

| 1 | 2 | 3 | 4 |

28 I use the same standard method of reporting progress to all stakeholders.

| 1 | 2 | 3 | 4 |

29 I prepare the objectives and agenda of meetings.

| 1 | 2 | 3 | 4 |

30 I use a logical process to make decisions with my project team.

| 1 | 2 | 3 | 4 |

31 I keep my sponsor fully up to date with progress on the project plan.

| 1 | 2 | 3 | 4 |

32 I use problem-solving techniques to arrive at decisions.

| 1 | 2 | 3 | 4 |

ANALYSIS

Now you have completed the self-assessment, add up your total score and check your performance by referring to the corresponding evaluation below. Whatever level of success you have achieved, there is always room for improvement. Identify your weakest areas and refer to the relevant sections to refine your skills.

32–64: You are not yet sufficiently well-organized to ensure that a complex project will achieve its objectives. Review the planning process thoroughly and make sure that you follow it through step-by-step.

65–95: You are a reasonably effective project manager, but need to address some weak points.

96–128: You are an excellent project manager. Be careful not to become complacent or to let your high standards slip.

INDEX

ACKNOWLEDGMENTS

AUTHORS' ACKNOWLEDGMENTS

There was an impressive team of skilled people involved in producing this book. In particular we would like to thank Adèle Hayward and Caroline Marklew of Dorling Kindersley for their help in sorting out the concepts, structure, and overall design of the book. Arthur Brown brought constructive and creative ideas to the detailed design stage, and Amanda Lebentz is the most positive and meticulous editor you could hope to have. We gratefully acknowledge their huge contributions.

PUBLISHER'S ACKNOWLEDGMENTS

Dorling Kindersley would like to thank the following for their help and participation in producing this book:

Photography Steve Gorton.

Models Roger Andre, Angela Cameron, Anne Chapman, Sander deGroot, Emma Harris, Lucy Kelly, Peter Taylor, Roberta Woodhouse.

Make-up Janice Tee.

Picture research Andy Sansom.
Picture library assistance Melanie Simmonds.

Indexer Hilary Bird.

PICTURE CREDITS

Key: *a* above, *b* bottom, *c* centre, *l* left, *r* right, *t* top

Stock Photolibrary/Zefa 2, 11 *t*; ... *bl*; Raoul Minsart 4; **Rex Interstock** Melanie/FOTEX front jacket; **Telegraph Colour Library** FPG/M Malyszko 64 *bl*; Ryanstock 19.

AUTHORS' BIOGRAPHIES

Andy Bruce is the founder of SofTools Limited – a specialist business research and consulting company. Following completion of a largely academic MBA programme, he has spent the past eight years helping a variety of organizations manage major projects and cope with change in the real world – more information on tools and techniques can be found at www.SofTools.net.

Ken Langdon has a background in sales and marketing in the computer industry. During his early years with a major computer supplier, he was involved in pioneering the use of project management techniques – including a comprehensive use of Pert – in the information technology departments of major computer users in industry and local government. As a consultant he has taught project planning techniques and assisted in the preparation of plans in the USA, Europe and Australasia.

Feminism: A Very Short Introduction

Very Short Introductions available now:

For more information visit our web site:
www.oup.co.uk/general/vsi/

Margaret Walters

FEMINISM

A Very Short Introduction

OXFORD

UNIVERSITY PRESS

OXFORD
UNIVERSITY PRESS

Great Clarendon Street, Oxford OX2 6DP

Oxford University Press is a department of the University of Oxford.
It furthers the University's objective of excellence in research, scholarship,
and education by publishing worldwide in

Oxford New York

Auckland Cape Town Dar es Salaam Hong Kong Karachi
Kuala Lumpur Madrid Melbourne Mexico City Nairobi
New Delhi Shanghai Taipei Toronto

With offices in

Argentina Austria Brazil Chile Czech Republic France Greece
Guatemala Hungary Italy Japan Poland Portugal Singapore
South Korea Switzerland Thailand Turkey Ukraine Vietnam

Oxford is a registered trade mark of Oxford University Press
in the UK and in certain other countries

Published in the United States
by Oxford University Press Inc., New York

© Margaret Walters 2005

British Library Cataloguing in Publication Data

Data available

Library of Congress Cataloging in Publication Data

Data available

ISBN 978-0-19-280510-2

9 10

Typeset by RefineCatch Ltd, Bungay, Suffolk
Printed in Great Britain by
Ashford Colour Press Ltd, Gosport, Hampshire

Contents

List of illustrations

The publisher and the author apologize for any errors or omissions in the above list. If contacted they will be pleased to rectify these at the earliest opportunity.

Introduction

'I myself have never been able to find out precisely what feminism is', the writer Rebecca West remarked, sardonically, in 1913. 'I only know that people call me a feminist whenever I express sentiments that differentiate me from a doormat or a prostitute.' The word was a comparatively new one when she wrote; it had only appeared in English – from the French – in the 1890s. Interestingly, the earliest examples of the word in the Oxford English Dictionary carried negative meanings. In 1895 the *Athenaeum* sneeringly referred to a piece about a woman whose 'coquetting with the doctrines of feminism' are traced with real humour. 'In Germany feminism is openly socialistic', the *Daily Chronicle* shuddered in 1908, and went on to dismiss out of hand 'suffragists, suffragettes and all the other phases in the crescendo of feminism'.

In those years, some writers used an alternative term – 'womanism' – with the same hostility. One long-forgotten writer was roused to angry sneers in his memoirs when he recalled meeting an intellectual woman living in Paris (she comes across, despite his prejudices, as lively and interesting) whose writings reflected 'the strong-minded womanism of the nineteenth century'.

Curiously, one of the sharpest attacks on the word 'feminism' came from Virginia Woolf, whose *A Room of One's Own* is such an effective and engaging plea for women. In *Three Guineas*, written in

1938 in the shadow of fascism and of approaching war, and probably nervous about any '-ism', she rejects the word out of hand. No one word can capture the force 'which in the nineteenth century opposed itself to the force of the fathers', she insists, continuing:

> Those nineteenth century women were in fact the advance guard of your own movement. They were fighting the tyranny of the patriarchal state as you are fighting the tyranny of the Fascist state.

They were called, to their resentment, feminists, she claims (she is historically inaccurate – the word was unknown in the previous century), and she goes on to insist that we must

> destroy an old word, a vicious and corrupt word that has done much harm in its day. The word 'feminist' is the word indicated. That word, according to the dictionary, means 'one who champions the rights of women.' Since the only right, the right to earn a living has been won, the word no longer has a meaning. And a word without a meaning is a dead word, a corrupt word.

But though Virginia Woolf's 'right to earn a living' was, and remains, central to feminism, getting on for a century after she wrote it is clear that its attainment by no means solved all women's problems. Women's work – despite the much-publicized earnings of some high-fliers in the business world – remains lower paid; or, in the case of housework, not paid at all. When Woolf was writing in the 1920s, feminists had hardly begun to articulate, let alone address, women's special problems: issues to do with childbirth and child-rearing, or the strain on women who had to combine housework and/or childcare with work outside the home.

Over the centuries, and in many different countries, women have spoken out for their sex, and articulated, in different ways, their complaints, their needs, and their hopes. As this is a Very Short Introduction, I have concentrated on feminism in one country,

England, and have tried to explore its development through time. While women in other countries have had different experiences and definitions, in England, right up until the 1960s at least, the word 'feminist' was usually pejorative. Very few women, however deeply engaged in fighting for women's rights, would have described themselves as 'feminists'. When women began to organize again in the 1960s and 1970s, the movement called itself Women's Liberation (borrowing the term from black, Third World, and student movements). This was often shortened, sometimes affectionately, sometimes in a derogatory way, to 'women's lib'. But those years also saw the word 'feminism' being brought back into general use, and its meaning was extended. Though there was still a justified concern that civil and legal equality had not been fully achieved, the new movement tended to concentrate on problems specific to women in their reproductive and social roles. In those years, too, feminists in Britain made an attempt, at least, to reach out across national boundaries and discover what they had – or did not have – in common with feminists abroad.

But how often, still, do we hear women anxiously asserting 'I'm not a feminist but . . . ' as they go on to make claims that depend upon, and would be impossible without, a feminist groundwork? The American feminist Estelle Freedman argues that right from its origins, the word has carried negative connotations; that surprisingly few politically engaged women have styled themselves feminists. In the 1990s some feminists in England and the United States identified and warned against a 'backlash' against feminism and its undoubted achievements. Juliet Mitchell and Ann Oakley, for example, called their third collection of essays *Who's Afraid of Feminism?*, with a cartoon of a big bad wolf on the original jacket cover. They argued that 'attacks on feminism frequently merge into a wider misogyny'; 'the feminist' is now the name given to the disliked or despised woman, much as 'man-hater' or 'castrating bitch', 'harridan' or 'witch', were used before the 1960s. They added that women also have to expose and eradicate the misogyny inherent in feminism itself.

3

Just as troubling is the caution that the term 'feminism' seems to arouse in many younger women, a surprising number of whom seem to shy away from the concept. One English tabloid recently published a double-page spread entitled 'Is Feminism Dead?', which managed, neatly enough, to sit on the fence; equal space was devoted to arguments yes and no, to those who felt the term was still urgently relevant, and to those who were sure it was dated, even embarrassing, and should be retired. The piece was illustrated with a photograph of 'militant women's libbers' picketing a Miss World demonstration. (In fact, everyone in the photo was laughing.) Faintly embarrassed, I recognized my much younger self, with long hair and long skirts, clutching a distinctly uninspired placard announcing that 'women are people too'. I had almost forgotten that the Miss World contests still existed (in those bad old days it was on prime-time television), until in 2002 the event received unexpected publicity, first when Nigerian militants demonstrated violently against its 'parade of nudity', which they thought would encourage promiscuity and Aids, then when several contestants refused to participate because a young Nigerian woman, sentenced to death under Islamic sharia law for having become pregnant outside marriage, was reprieved – but only until she had weaned her baby. The beauty queens' gesture was both courageous and effective, though interestingly, one insisted, with a hint of anxiety, that she took up her stand, certainly not because she was a feminist, or even because she was a woman, but because she was a human being.

When I recently asked some women in their early 20s – some of whom were university-educated, others working, and all, clearly, beneficiaries of earlier battles for women's rights – whether they considered themselves feminists, or indeed had any interest in feminism, most of them replied, flatly, no. The very term itself, one woman claimed, sounds stuffy and out of date. Feminism, she felt, has become, on the one hand, a playground for extremists – she termed them 'fundamentalists' – who had nothing useful to say to women like herself. On the other hand, she argued, feminism has become 'institutionalized', and she compared it to communism: it demands commitment, not simply to ideas, but to a generalized ideology. Moreover, she added, it is nowadays just another academic subject. You can get a degree in 'gender studies' and that, she felt, is the real kiss of death: proof, if any were needed, that feminism is no longer urgently relevant. Perhaps these younger women will feel differently in ten years or so, when they find themselves juggling family, housework, and a job; perhaps they will find that they need to re-invent feminism to suit their own experience. But in a way, I hope they will not need to.

Chapter 1
The religious roots
of feminism

Some of the first European women to speak out for themselves, and for their sex, did so within a religious framework, and in religious terms. It is perhaps not always easy, in our secular society, to bring them back to life: to recognize fully their courage, or to understand the implications, or the extent, of their challenge to the status quo.

For centuries, and all over Europe, there were families who disposed of 'unnecessary' or unmarriageable daughters by shutting them away in convents. For some, this must have felt like life imprisonment; but for others, conventual quiet seems to have facilitated genuine fulfilment: it allowed some women to develop a talent for organization, and some were able to read and think, and discover their own distinctive voices. Hildegard of Bingen, who was born at the end of the 11th century and became a nun, and later the abbess, of a small Rhineland convent, has long been known as a remarkable and impressive writer; recently, her great musical talent has been rediscovered and celebrated. But she was sometimes plagued with doubts about her 'unfeminine' activities, and wrote to one of the leading churchmen of the time, Bernard of Clairvaux, asking if she – an uneducated woman – should continue with her writing and with composing. He encouraged her, and within a few years she was known and honoured all over Europe. When she was 60 years old, she embarked upon preaching tours all through the

German empire, even though at that time only priests were allowed to preach.

Like other medieval women, when seeking to imagine the almost unimaginable, and to communicate her understanding of God's love, she turned to womanly, and specifically maternal, experience, and wrote of the 'motherhood' of God. 'God showed me his grace again', she writes, 'as . . . when a mother offers her weeping child milk.' Some religious women imagine, with maternal tenderness, the infant Jesus. A Flemish Beguine meditates on what the mother of God must have felt:

> for three or more days [she] held Him close to her so that He nestled between her breasts like a baby . . . sometimes she kissed him as though he were a little child and sometimes she held Him on her lap as if He were a gentle lamb.

'Just because I am a woman, must I therefore believe that I must not tell you about the goodness of God . . . ?' asked the Englishwoman Julian of Norwich in the early 15th century. She marvelled that 'he who was her Maker chose to be born of the creature that is made'. Moreover, she argued:

> our Saviour is our true mother in whom we are eternally born and by whom we shall always be enclosed . . . We are redeemed by the motherhood of mercy and grace . . . to the nature of motherhood belong tender love, wisdom and knowledge, and it is good, for although the birth of our body is only low, humble and modest compared with the birth of our soul, yet it is he who does it in the beings by women it was done.

Whereas other women had made the analogy briefly, Julian of Norwich goes on to spell out the comparison very directly. Christ is like

> the kind, loving mother who knows and recognizes the need of her

child, and carefully watches over it. The mother can give her child milk to suck, but our dear mother Jesus can feed us with himself, and he does so most generously and most tenderly . . .

Margery Kempe, a contemporary of Julian's who travelled from her Essex home to visit her, produced an account of her own life – probably dictated to a scribe – that has been described as the first autobiography in English. Her life story reveals, only too clearly, why her self-preoccupation and her melodramatic acting out of her own miseries infuriated so many people who came into contact with her. But her story is also, unexpectedly, a deeply touching one; and more than that, it is impressive simply because she insists on taking herself and her experiences seriously. Margery came up against the painful and terrible aspect of the motherhood that had inspired the celibate Julian. She was miserably ill all through her first pregnancy, and after a prolonged and very painful birth, was left exhausted and depressed: 'what with the labour she had in childbirthing and the sicknesse going before, she despaired of her life'. At times, she came near to killing herself. She was comforted, she recalls, by a vision of Christ, in the form of a handsome young man sitting at her bedside; he informed her that 'you may boldly, when you are in bed, take me to you as your wedded husband'. But it was only years later, and after 14 pregnancies, that Margery finally managed to negotiate a deal with her demanding mortal husband: if he stopped insisting on sex, she would pay off his debts, and forgo her strict Friday fast to eat and drink with him. He agreed, though with a hint of sarcasm that echoes nastily across the centuries: 'May your body be as freely available to God as it has been to me.'

With remarkable energy and determination, Margery then set out across Europe on a pilgrimage, and though her constant weeping and wailing so infuriated her fellow pilgrims that they abandoned her en route, her courage – and obsessive determination – enabled her to reach Jerusalem, and eventually to get as far as Constantinople.

By the late 16th century, increasing numbers of women were beginning to argue their case more consistently and more aggressively, though still within a religious framework. The Reformation enabled more women to receive an education. In 1589, in what one historian has called 'the earliest piece of English feminist polemic', Jane Anger took up a challenging position by insisting that Eve was superior to Adam: a second, and hence improved, model. Whereas Adam was fashioned from 'dross and filthy clay', God made Eve from Adam's flesh, 'that she might be purer than he', which 'doth evidently show how far we women are more excellent than men . . . From woman sprang man's salvation. A woman was the first that believed, and a woman likewise the first that repented of sin.' Anger then descends crossly, and comically, to everyday domestic life. It is women, she reminds us, who make sure that men are fed, clothed, and cleaned: 'without our care they lie in their beds as dogs in litter, and go like lousy mackerel swimming in the heat of summer'.

But any woman wanting to defend her sex had to tackle powerfully negative scriptural images of women: Delilah was treacherous, Jezebel murderous, while Eve was directly responsible for the Fall of the human race: 'the woman tempted him and he did eat'. Saint Paul was regularly invoked against any woman who spoke out, or asked awkward questions about the Church's attitude to women: 'Let your women keep silence in the churches, for it is not permitted to them to speak', he instructed the Corinthians. And again, in the epistle to Timothy, 'if they will learn anything let them ask their husbands at home: for it is shame for women to speak in the church'.

Gradually, a few women found the confidence to defy these scriptural prohibitions. Some offered dissenting interpretations of Genesis, arguing that Adam was, after all, as much to blame for the Fall as Eve. So, in 1611, Aemilia Lanyer reminded her readers that Christ was begotten of a woman, born of a woman, nourished of a woman, obedient to a woman ... he healed women, pardoned women, comforted women ... after his resurrection, appeared first to a woman.

And Rachel Speght sardonically remarked in 1617:

If Adam had not approved that deed which Eve had done, and been willing to tread the steps which she had gone, he being her head would have reproved her, have made the commandment a bit to restrain him from breaking his master's position.

Others insisted that God had signalled his forgiveness by making Mary, a descendant of Eve, the mother of Christ.

In the course of the troubled 17th century, particularly among the sects, the many and various small groups that rejected the established Church in favour of purer forms of worship, women found more freedom. Some, at least, felt inspired to preach or to prophesy. Modern historians have pointed out the important role of women among the religious separatists who fled persecution in late Elizabethan England by emigrating to America or to Holland, as well as their activity as preachers. Women were active, too, among the small dissenting groups that managed to survive underground in England, until, during the Civil War and Interregnum, they emerged dramatically and vocally. Keith Thomas lists some of these independent congregations: Brownists, Independents, Baptists, Millenarians, Familists, Quakers, Seekers, Ranters. Whatever their theological differences, they all believed the necessity for spiritual regeneration in *every* individual. The experiencing of what Quakers called the 'Inner Light' was more important than external observance – and that light knows no sexual distinction. As one contemporary writer claimed, 'one faithful man, yea, or woman either, may as truly and effectually loose and bind, both in heaven and earth, as all the ministers in the world'.

Various independent congregations had, for some time, been allowing women to debate publicly and to vote on matters of Church business; by the 1640s some, particularly among the Quakers, were going further. In 1659, the Quaker Fox argued that 'Christ is in the male as in the female, who redeems from under the Law . . . Christ in the male and female, who are in the spirit of God, are not under the Law.'

'Might not the spirit of Christ, that is begotten of God in the female as well as the male . . . speak?' asked Katherine Evans and Sarah Chevers. Increasingly often, women felt moved, divinely inspired, to speak in meetings and even at service, though they were often greeted with bitter opposition. They were criticized for being 'puffed up with pride' and 'vainglorious arrogance', and even worse, for 'usurping authority over men'. In 1646, for example, John Vicars complained bitterly about 'bold impudent housewives . . . without all womanly modesty who take upon them . . . to prate . . . most directly contrary to the apostle's inhibition'.

John Bunyan was totally opposed to this active participation by women, arguing that Satan, inevitably, tempts the weaker Eve, rather than Adam: 'the man was made the head in worship, and the keeper of the garden of God'. He referred to women as 'that simple and weak sex'. Citing the first epistle to the Corinthians, he argued that women are 'not the image and glory of God as the men are. They are placed beneath.' He disapproved of separate women's meetings, which did nothing but encourage 'unruliness'. 'I do not believe they [women] should minister to God in prayer before the whole church,' he insisted, adding sarcastically, 'for then I should be a Ranter or a Quaker.' In any public gathering, 'her part is to hold her tongue, to learn in silence'.

Even in the 1670s, that courageous Quaker Margaret Fell still felt the need to defend women's independence of conscience, and their right to play an active part in worship. In a tract called *Women's Speaking Justified*, she argued emphatically: 'Those that speak

11

1. The scene is viewed with a hint of satire – though is it directed at the earnest speaker or at the inattentive audience? One is actually sleeping, others demonstrate disapproval.

against . . . the spirit of the Lord speaking in a woman, simply by reason of her sex . . . speak against Christ and his Church, and are of the Seed of the Serpent.'

The prophet Joel was sometimes cited as an answer to Saint Paul's prohibition spirit upon all flesh:

12

> . . . and your sons and your daughters shall prophesy, your old men
> shall dream dreams, your young men shall see visions: And also
> upon the servants and upon the handmaids in those days will I pour
> out my spirit. And I will shew wonders in the heavens and in the
> earth, blood and fire, and pillars of smoke.

Joel's ecstatic vision seemed, to many, particularly relevant during
the great upheavals caused by the Civil War and the Interregnum;
there was a widespread feeling that apocalypse was, indeed,
imminent. The sect who styled themselves Fifth Monarchists, for
example, believed that the world's four great secular empires –
Babylon, Persia, Greece, and Rome – having passed away, the fifth –
Christ's Kingdom and the rule of the saints – was close at hand. In
this feverish and volatile climate, prophets, many with
revolutionary ideas, flourished.

In this area, a woman's supposed passivity, her receptivity to
outside influence, could, ironically, be claimed as an advantage:
she might prove more receptive, more open, to becoming a channel
for the voice of God. The Belgian prophet Antonia Bourigue,
who was widely read in England, produced a disconcerting and
double-edged justification: 'they ought to let God speak by a
woman, if it be His Pleasure, since he spoke in former times to a
Prophet by a Beast'.

But the line between prophetic inspiration and lunacy, between
possession by God and by the devil, was a narrow one. In
17th-century England, women were still being tried for witchcraft.
Moreover, female prophets could easily be dismissed as merely
crazy. Lady Eleanor Davis, for example, had been claiming divine
inspiration for years; early one morning in 1625, she heard 'a Voice
from Heaven, speaking as through a trumpet these words, There is
nineteen years and a half to the Judgement Day'. She went on to
publish tracts that were interpreted as predicting, amongst other
things, the death of Charles I. Her husband burned her books; and
she was often the butt of jokes. An anagram of her name – *Dame*

13

Eleanor Davis: Never so mad a ladie – was gleefully circulated. But her visionary fervour put her at real risk; even her rank could not protect her from charges of treachery. In 1633, after being charged before the High Commission that 'she took upon her (which much unbeseemed her sex) not only to interpret the Scriptures . . . but also to be a prophetess', she was fined and imprisoned in Bedlam. But she came into her own during the Interregnum, when many of her prophecies seemed to have been realized. She went on to publish at least 37 tracts between 1641 and her death 11 years later.

Another prophetess, Anna Trapnel, experienced some kind of revelation at a Baptist church in London. By 1652, she had joined the Fifth Monarchists, and in 1654, she accompanied a male preacher to Whitehall, where she fell into a trance that lasted for 12 days. Crowds gathered to hear her prophecies – and her harsh criticisms of Oliver Cromwell and his government – which were recorded in *Strange and Wonderful News from Whitehall* and *The Cry of a Stone*. She insisted – in verse – that God's message was addressed to women as well as men:

> John though wilt not offended be
> That handmaids here should sing,
> That they should meddle to declare
> The matters of the King . . . .

The authorities labelled her as mad, but still brought her to trial. 'The report was that I would discover myself to be a witch when I came before the justices, by having never a word to answer for myself', she said. But her sheer volubility defeated the court, and she continued, undeterred, with her prophecies. Cromwell's government undoubtedly took this kind of prediction seriously; several times, he and his council were interrupted by, and seriously listened to, prophets, several of whom were women.

The appeal to divine inspiration was probably of limited value as a means of female emancipation; the feminism of the future would depend less on the assertion of women's spiritual equality and more on natural rights, and a denial that there is any intellectual difference between the sexes.

But there were political implications to this outburst of religious fervour. In the 16th century, the Anabaptists had recognized women as equal to men, and allowed them to pray and speak in meetings. Women from the congregations who styled themselves Levellers seem to have been particularly active on a larger stage, and showed considerable political shrewdness. The sect encouraged women's activity, believing in the equality of all 'made in the image of God'. In the 1640s and early 1650s, when many of their husbands were in prison, Leveller women repeatedly turned up en masse at Westminster – staging what sounds very like contemporary 'demonstrations' – to demand freedom for their husbands, but also to complain bitterly about their own, consequent hardships. They were usually treated harshly, and rebuked for meddling in things beyond their understanding. The crowds of women who petitioned for peace in 1642 and 1643 were dismissed contemptuously as 'Whores, Bawds, Oyster women, Kitchen maids'. Three hundred women, who presented another petition to the House of Lords, were rejected out of hand by the Duke of Lennox. 'Away with these women,' he exclaimed, adding, with a jeer, 'we were best have a Parliament of women.' In May 1649 yet another petition for the release of the Leveller prisoners was turned away sarcastically: 'It was not for women to Petition, they might stay at home and wash the dishes.' To which the women, unabashed, retorted, 'we have scarcely any dishes left us to wash'.

Later in that year, they tried again. As many as ten thousand women signed yet another petition, asking:

> We cannot but wonder and grieve that we should appear so despicable in your eyes as to be thought unworthy to petition to represent our grievances to this honourable House. Have we not an equal interest with the men of this nation in those liberties and

securities contained in the Petition of Right, and other good laws of the land? Are any of our lives, limbs, liberties or goods to be taken from us, no more than from men, but by due process of law . . .

A thousand women carried it to the House with sea-green ribbons pinned to their breasts. Once again, they were dismissed scornfully.

But among the Quakers, particularly, women found the chance to develop their skills as administrators. Regular women's meetings were set up alongside the men's meetings in the 1650s; and though, from the beginning, women seem to have concentrated on traditionally feminine areas, such as welfare and moral problems, they had the chance to develop their own, very effective organization, which in fact handled considerable sums of money. However, historians have suggested that there was a gradual reduction in the scope of their concerns; by the 1680s, they were confining themselves to 'womanly' matters. In these later years, they concentrated on 'such things as are proper to us, as the poor more especially and the destitute amongst us'. These included helping young men to find apprenticeships or work, and instructing younger women 'to all wholesome things', which included looking after their husbands, children, and homes, and always behaving in a manner that was 'discreet, chaste, and sober'.

Chapter 2
The beginning of
secular feminism

Secular self-assertion, perhaps inevitably, developed more slowly; it was one thing to act in 'unfeminine' ways if divinely inspired, not quite so easy to act unconventionally out of personal ambition. Speaking in public, or writing, was all very well when it was in the Lord's cause, and could be claimed as the product of divine inspiration: 'I am a very weak and unworthy woman . . . I could do no more of myself than a pencil or pen can do when no hand guides it', acknowledged one 17th-century female author. Moreover, many women, Quakers and members of other sects, obviously gained confidence from being part of a supportive community with whom they shared beliefs and values.

Worldly ambition was something else. There had of course been, within living memory of many, a great queen of England, who was learned and well read. Working with the scholar Roger Ascham, Elizabeth became fluent in Latin, Greek, and French; he remarked, approvingly, that 'her mind has no womanly weakness, her perseverance is equal to that of a man'. But for all her self-assertiveness, she was hardly supportive of other women. Her famous speech to the troops at Tilbury in (1588) made a sharp distinction between her role as woman and as monarch: 'I know I have the body but of a weak and feeble woman, but I have the heart and stomach of a king, and a king of England too.' But her mere existence was probably an encouragement, at least, to some

Englishwomen, to trust in their own talents, and to accept their own 'unfeminine' ambition. There were certainly Royalist women who – in the absence of their husbands during the Civil War – struggled bravely to defend their families and homes. Anne Bradstreet (an English-born poet who later emigrated to America) wrote, 40 years after the Queen's death:

> Let such as say our sex is void of reason
> Know 'tis a slander now, but once was Treason.

An anonymous work entitled *The Woman's Sharpe Revenge* (1640) argued, provocatively, that women's exclusion from learning was 'devised by men to secure their own continued domination'. Bathsua Makin, who was governess to a daughter of Charles I and who later founded and ran a school for women, insisted in her *Essay to Revive the Ancient Education of Gentlewomen in Religion, Manners, Arts and Tongues* on the importance of women receiving a solid education. 'Let women be fools', she remarked, 'and you will make them slaves.' Her book was probably, in part at least, an advertisement for her school and its curriculum; and it was aimed at well-off women. Interestingly, she offered women the (still rare) chance to study the classics. But she reassured her readers by making it clear that she would not 'hinder good housewifery, neither have I called any from their necessary labour to the book'. And, with a hint of anxiety, she insists that 'my intention is not to equalize women to men, much less to make them superior. They are the weaker sex.'

But Bathsua Makin warmly praised the role played by Royalist women during the Civil War: they 'defended their houses and did all things, as soldiers, with prudence and valour, like men'. And she was generously appreciative of her learned contemporaries, including Anne Bradstreet and the Duchess of Newcastle. The biblical story of how Eve brought sin into the world by eating the forbidden apple, so often used against women, is, Makin argues, merely the earliest example of a need for adequate education.

Christine de Pizan

Christine de Pizan, born in 14th-century Italy but raised in France, has been described as the first Western woman to live by her pen. Well educated by her father, she began writing aged 25, after her husband died, earning enough to support three children, a niece, and her own mother. Her most famous work, *The City of Ladies* (1404), criticizes learned books that spread 'so many wicked insults about women and their behaviour'; three allegorical women – Reason, Rectitude, and Justice – discuss the roots of misogyny. 'The man or the woman in whom resides greater virtue is the higher', she argued; 'neither the loftiness nor the lowliness of a person lies in the body according to the sex, but in the perfection of conduct and virtues.'

In 1599 Marguerite de Navarre published the *Heptaméron*, defending women against misogynous attacks. Marie de Gournay's *Egalité des hommes et des femmes* (1622) asserted women's intellectual equality with men: 'happy are you, Reader, if you do not belong to this sex to which all good is forbidden'. And in 1640, Anne Marie van Schurmann's *On the Capacity of the Female Mind for Learning* insisted that 'whatever fills the human mind with uncommon and honest delight is fitting for a human woman'.

Many early secular writers seem to have had a hard time. In 1621 Lady Mary Wroth (a niece of the poet Sir Philip Sidney) was engaged in writing a sonnet sequence, which she left unfinished. It was not printed until the 20th century, when women literary critics analysed the interesting and refreshing slant she brought to that usually intensely masculine form. But when Wroth had the temerity to *publish* a prose romance, *The Countess of Montgomery's Urania*, it was greeted with hostility, and, on the grounds that it slandered contemporaries, withdrawn from sale. Her rank offered no protection. 'Work, Lady, work,' Lord Denny advised Lady Mary, condescendingly, 'let writing books alone/For surely wiser women ne'er wrote one.'

The difficulties – indeed, the outspoken scorn – confronting any woman who actually dared to publish her writings are clearly indicated by the experiences of Margaret Cavendish, Duchess of Newcastle. Born into a family of well-established, Royalist East Anglian landowners, she went to court as a young woman, then accompanied Queen Henrietta Maria into exile in Paris, where she met and married the Marquess, later the Duke, of Newcastle. Her privileges – rank and riches – certainly protected her; but they also, along with her flamboyantly eccentric personal style and, most of all, her unconcealed literary ambition, made her an easy target for malicious and denigrating gossip. She was fortunate in her marriage; the Duke, much older than his wife, encouraged her endeavours, and, after one of the many attacks on her work, remarked: 'Here's the crime, a lady writes them, and to entrench so much upon the male prerogative is not to be forgiven.'

Though her situation was, in many respects, very different from that of most other women, she wrote very movingly about women's common fears and griefs, particularly about their children: 'the care for their well being, the fear for their ill doing, the grief for their sickness and their unsufferable sorrow for their death'. These were concerns that might afflict any woman, whatever her status.

Cavendish began to write philosophical verse when she and her husband returned to London; as a modern biographer remarks, she felt torn between 'the (feminine and Christian) virtue of modesty' and her own ambitions. She rightly took her work very seriously, but she was often forced to retreat into defensive, and self-deprecating, justifications. Writing was, she remarked apologetically, the 'harmlessest pastime' for leisured women; much better than, say, sitting around gossiping about the neighbours. It was a 'proper and virtuous' activity, and men who disapproved, she argued, should hope their own wives and daughters 'may employ the time no worse than in honest, innocent and harmless fancies'.

However, Cavendish certainly never regarded her own work as harmless fancy. Though she was critical of the exclusive arrogance of the Universities of Cambridge and Oxford, she courageously dedicated two books to them. In 1653, when she published *Poems and Fancies*, she claimed that she wrote because 'all heroic actions, public employments, powerful governments and eloquent pleadings are denied our sex in this age . . . '. The implication being that writing in itself may be a heroic activity; and for any woman of her generation, it probably was. Moreover, in her 1655 *Philosophical and Physical Opinions*, she complained that

> we are kept like birds in cages to hop up and down in our houses, not suffered to fly abroad . . . we are shut out of all power and authority, by reason we are never employed either in civil or martial affairs, our counsels are despised and laughed at, the best of our actions are trodden down with scorn, by the overweening conceit men have of themselves and through despisement of us.

But in nature, she argued in the preface to *The World's Olio*, written when she first returned to London but published in 1655, 'we have as clear an understanding as men, if we were bred in schools to mature our brains and to mature our knowledge'.

But for all her ambition and her persistence, she had few illusions and sometimes, inevitably perhaps, her courage failed her; she gloomily predicted readers' responses to her autobiographical *True Relation*: 'Why hath this lady writ her own life, since none cares to know whose daughter she was or whose wife she is, or how she was bred, or what fortunes she had, or how she lived?'

2. Margaret Cavendish, Duchess of Newcastle, was an intellectually astute writer who spoke out eloquently against the hostility directed at any woman regarded as outspoken or ambitious.

And, indeed, readers were often unkind. The diarist Samuel Pepys, intensely and maliciously curious, spent weeks in 1667 tracking her around London, then, after reading her life of her husband, condemned her as 'a mad, conceited, ridiculous woman'. And though Cavendish hopefully dedicated two prefaces specifically to women readers, urging them to spend time 'on anything that may bring honour to our sex, for they are poor, dejected spirits that are not ambitious of fame', she admitted that convention, in constraining women's talents, made them jealously critical of each other's achievements, and that she would probably 'be censured by my own sex'. As she often was. Her contemporary Dorothy Osborne's response to Newcastle's *Poems and Fancies* is sadly revealing about the extent of disapproving prejudice – even amongst intelligent women – against women's writing. Dorothy was enjoyably shocked when she heard about the Duchess's book, and wrote to her fiancé, Sir William Temple:

> For God's sake, if you meet with it, send it me; they say 'tis ten times more extravagant than her dress. Sure, the poor woman is a little distracted, she could never be so ridiculous else as to venture at writing books, and in verse too. If I should not sleep this fortnight I should not come to that.

She wrote again shortly afterwards, telling Temple not to bother, as she had already obtained and read the book, ' . . . and am satisfied that there are many soberer people in Bedlam'. But, ironically and rather sadly, Osborne's own letters to her fiancé reveal a lively, observant, articulate woman; as Virginia Woolf remarked, 'what a gift that untaught and solitary girl had for the framing of a sentence, for the fashioning of a scene'. In another age, she implies, Osborne might have made a novelist.

Intriguingly, the seedy and cynical world of Restoration London provided some unexpected opportunities for women. They might work as actresses, though that was hardly a socially respectable profession; they were often treated as if they were, in essence, merely prostitutes. But in addition, a number of women emerged as playwrights: Catherine Trotter, Mary Manley, and Mary Pix all had plays produced – and were cruelly mocked in a play by a certain 'W. M.' which was staged in 1696. Mary Manley, in the prologue to her first play, foresaw the difficulties they would all face:

The Curtain's drawn now by a Lady's hand
The very name you'll cry bodes Impotence,
To Fringe and Tea they should confine their sense.

Aphra Behn is the best-known of these women who were finding the courage to break new ground, and to face down this kind of jeering criticism. Virginia Woolf glimpsed something of Behn's importance, describing her as

> a middle class woman with all the plebeian virtues of humour, vitality and courage; a woman forced by the death of her husband and some unfortunate adventures of her own to make her living by her wits, she had to work on equal terms with men. She made, by working very hard, enough to live on. The importance of that fact outweighs anything she actually wrote.

More recent readers have taken what Behn 'actually wrote' much more seriously – she was a skilful and often challenging dramatist – while some critics have found her life almost as interesting as her plays. Before becoming a writer, she had travelled widely – perhaps to Surinam in South America; certainly, as a government spy, to the Low Countries. Though she is best known as a playwright, she also penned *Love-Letters Between a Nobleman and His Sister*. A recent biographer has convincingly argued that this neglected tale is in fact a great erotic novel, which is also a profound exploration of the potency and the perils of romantic fantasy.

She was often attacked – as male playwrights were not – for bawdiness. Alexander Pope was the most famous of those who sneered at her immorality: 'The stage how loosely doth Astraea tread/ Who fairly puts all characters to bed.' Behn defended herself eloquently:

> Had the plays I have writ come forth under any man's name, and never known to have been mine; I appeal to all unbiased judges of sense if they had not said that person had made as good comedies, as

any one man that has writ in our age; but a devil on't the woman damns the poet ... I value fame as much as if I had been born a hero.

In fact, a play like *The Rover* is a cool, clear-eyed analysis of how women have to manoeuvre, negotiate – and inevitably compromise – in their dealings with men, who are portrayed, almost uniformly, as cold-hearted exploiters. Behn's heroine Hellena – through a combination of luck, wit, shrewd calculation, and skill at role-playing – achieves respectability (though almost certainly not happiness) in marriage to the predatory Willmore. But there are hints that Behn may have sympathized most, and perhaps even identified, not with the (more or less) virtuous Hellena, but with the whore Angellica Bianca. As modern critics have pointed out, the heroine and her creator share the same initials. Angellica, ironically, is at heart an idealist, and as such alone among a cast of cynics and manipulators. She believes her seducer's fine romantic words, and at the close of the play she is excluded, left bitter and disillusioned. Behn's ending leaves us disconcerted, uncomfortable, questioning, for Behn's sympathies, and ours, are undoubtedly with the hapless Angellica. In a postscript defending her play against charges of plagiarism (women were especially vulnerable to dismissive sneers about their ability), Behn admitted that though she might 'have stoln some hints' from an earlier work by Thomas Killigrew, 'the Plot and Bus'ness (not to boast on't) is my own'. And she continued with an ambiguous statement that seems to confirm some kind of personal identification with her unhappy character: 'I, vainly proud of my judgement, hang out the Sign of Angellica (the only stoln Object) to give Notice where a great part of the Wit dwelt.'

Chapter 3
The 18th century:
Amazons of the pen

Mary Astell was one of the earliest true feminists, perhaps the first English writer to explore and assert ideas about women which we can still recognize and respond to. Throughout her life she identified with and spoke directly to other women, acknowledging their shared problems. Though she was deeply religious, she had little in common with her outspoken predecessors in the 17th-century sects. She was profoundly conservative; a life-long Royalist and a High Church Anglican, radical only in her perception of the way women's lives were restricted by convention, and their minds left undeveloped and untrained.

Astell was born in 1666. Her father, a Newcastle coal merchant, died when she was 12 years old. In her late teens, Astell fell into a deep depression, writing poems about her lonely misery, and the fact that, for all her intellectual self-confidence, she could not envisage any tolerable future for herself. At the age of 21, she wrote a poem complaining about her frustration (which must have been shared by many other girls) and gloomily admitting that she could imagine no life that would allow her to use her talents or satisfy her ambition.

> Nature permits not me the common way,
> By serving Court or State, to gain
> That so much valu'd trifle fame

She might, perhaps, have found satisfaction as a missionary:

> That to the Turk and Infidel
> I might the joyfull tydings tell
> And spare no labour to convert them all
> But ah my Sex denies me this . . .

But a few months later, in what was surely an act of remarkable courage, she left home, setting out on the long and uncomfortable journey to London with only a little money, and the addresses of a few family contacts. She seems to have settled in Chelsea from the start, and would remain there for the rest of her life; she had some distant relatives there. But they were not very helpful, and she was soon depressed and unable to see any way forward. In 1688, desperate because she was 'not able to get a liflyhood', she wrote to William Sancroft, Archbishop of Canterbury, asking for help:

> For since GOD has given Women as well as Men intelligent Souls, how should they be forbidden to improve them? Since he has not denied us the faculty of Thinking, why should we not (at least in gratitude to him) employ our Thoughts on himself their noblest Object, and not unworthily bestow them on Trifles and Gaities and secular Affairs?

Archbishop Sancroft, obviously impressed by her intelligence, and piety, responded with money, but, more importantly, with contacts. Before long, Mary Astell had come to know a circle of intelligent women, who became her life-long friends, sympathizing with and supporting her ideas. By 1694, she had written and published her first book, *A Serious Proposal to the Ladies*, urging other women to take themselves seriously: they must learn to think for themselves, work to develop their own minds and skills, rather than always deferring to masculine judgement. One of her books was entitled *Thoughts on Education*; her work was pioneering, genuinely seminal – and it remains interesting because of her stress on the urgent necessity for women to be properly educated. Girls, she argued, must be taught to think for themselves, to judge clearly and sensibly, rather than waste all their time in acquiring graceful social skills and accomplishments.

> We value them [men] too much and our selves too little, if we place any part of our desert in their Opinion, and don't think our selves capable of Nobler Things than the pitiful Conquest of some worthless Heart.

Astell always wrote clearly and sharply, often with an edge of wit: 'your glass will not do you half so much service as a serious reflection on your own Minds'.

Astell's analysis was certainly timely. Some modern historians have argued that the Reformation, and especially the closure of many convents, had actually made it harder for English women to get any kind of education. But women, Astell argued, were just as capable as men; all they lacked was a rigorous training that would 'cultivate and improve them'. She generously supported other women, warmly praising, for example, Lady Mary Wortley Montagu's collection of correspondence and travel writing, *Turkish Letters*:

> Let her own Sex at least do her Justice ... let us freely own the Superiority of the Sublime Genius as I do in the sincerity of my Soul, pleas'd that a *Woman* triumphs, and proud to follow in her train.

But 'what poor Woman is ever taught that she should have a higher Design than to get her a Husband?' she asked in her 1700 book *Some Reflections Upon Marriage*. She admitted, rather reluctantly, that marriage was necessary to propagate the species, but insisted that a wife is all too often simply 'a Man's Upper Servant'. Any woman who 'does not practice Passive Obedience to the utmost will never be acceptable to such an absolute Sovereign as a Husband', she warned. She had sketched her own ideal in her first book: a secular convent, where women could live together, retired from the world, in happy and studious innocence, 'such a paradise as your mother *Eve* forfeited'. Adam would have no place in this Eden. In

Some Reflections, she developed the suggestion in greater and more practical detail, arguing the need for women's colleges that would provide them, whatever their future, with a thorough education. Perhaps even more important to her, these colleges would also help unmarried women; they might, in fact, offer some women the choice of a life that was not dependent upon men.

As she became better known, Astell was often the target of mockery and crude lampoons: she eventually stopped writing, but was able to use her influence in very effective ways. In 1709, he persuaded some of her wealthier Chelsea acquaintances to support the opening of a charity school. Her project was timely: between May 1699 and 1704, fifty-four schools had already been set up in London and Westminster; by 1729, there were 132 in this area, and many women were becoming deeply involved in their planning and management; and, gradually, in teaching.

Astell's consistently and austerely negative attitudes towards men and marriage undoubtedly limited her appeal for many women readers. But her great contribution to feminism was the way she urged women to take themselves seriously, to trust in their own judgement, to make their own choices in life by developing their talents and educating themselves. Her own achievements, she insisted, were not in any way exceptional; she had 'not the least Reason to imagine that her Understanding is any better than the rest of her Sex'. Any difference arose only from 'her Application, her Disinterested and Unprejudic'd Love to Truth, and unswerving pursuit of it, notwithstanding all Discouragements, which is in every Womans Power'.

It was only towards the end of the 18th century that other women would speak out as clearly and forcefully, or put forward a comparable, and as powerfully feminist, programme. But through the 18th century, the situation of women was changing, not always favourably. In an increasingly bourgeois society, fewer women were working alongside their husbands in family workshops or businesses. It was perhaps harder for women to live independently, supporting themselves; and, it has been suggested, it was much harder to find a husband without a dowry. At the same time, far more women were being educated, at least to read and write. All through the century, 'conduct' books were addressed directly to women, though they mostly recommended the 'womanly' virtues of meekness, piety, and charity, and all stressed the central importance of modesty, which was often used as a polite synonym for chastity. But more women themselves were also writing and publishing, and in many different genres; they were numerous enough, indeed, to annoy the great Dr Johnson, who took time out to mock the new 'Amazons of the pen'.

The greatest of these feminist 'Amazons' was Mary Wollstonecraft. Her *Vindication of the Rights of Woman* was published in 1792, and still speaks directly to us. But she was by no means alone. Catherine Macaulay, for example, was, like Wollstonecraft, a radical who responded thoughtfully to the Revolution in France. She had already published a many-volumed *History of England* when, in 1790, she wrote *Letters on Education*, arguing, as Wollstonecraft would do a little later, that women's apparent weaknesses were not natural, but simply the product of mis-education. Macaulay also attacked the sexual double standard, insisting that a single sexual experience does not transform a virgin into a wanton. She firmly rejected the notion that women were 'the mere property of the men', with no right to dispose of their own persons.

She certainly alarmed some readers; as one man remarked dismissively to a woman friend, 'once in every age I would wish such a woman to appear, as proof that genius is not confined to sex . . . but . . . you'll pardon me, we want no more than *one* Mrs. Macaulay'. Even a sympathetic reader like John Adams, the future American president, praised her, ambiguously, as 'a Lady of masculine masterly understanding'. Mary Wollstonecraft knew Macaulay's work, and sent her a copy of her own *Vindication of the Rights of Men*, along with a letter remarking that 'you are the only female writer who I coincide in opinion with respecting the rank our sex ought to endeavour to attain in the world'. 'I will not call hers a masculine understanding', Wollstonecraft wrote, 'because I admit not such an arrogant assumption of reason; but I contend that it was a sound one, and that her judgement . . . was a proof that a woman can acquire judgement in the full extent of the word.' She valued Macaulay, she continued, because she 'contends for laurels' while most women 'only seek for flowers'.

Mary Wollstonecraft was born in 1759, to a not very successful would-be middle-class family; her early life is a chilling reminder of how little education was available to girls in that period. Most girls were taught at home – rarely very satisfactorily – either by their mothers, or by poorly trained governesses. In the later part of the century, private schools for middle-class girls flourished, but many simply concentrated on helping their pupils to be graceful and well-mannered, readying them for 'good' marriages. Wollstonecraft had briefly attended a day school in Yorkshire, but she was essentially self-educated. At one point a neighbouring clergyman lent her books, and she seems to have studied them rigorously, allowing herself nothing 'for mere amusement, not even poetry', but 'concentrating instead on works which are addressed to the understanding'.

Like so many skimpily educated girls in her day, she found it hard to earn a living. She took a post in Bath as companion to an old lady when she was 19 years old, then came home to nurse her dying mother; later she scraped a living by taking in needlework. With her sisters and her closest friend Fanny Blood, she set up a school in Newington Green, which soon failed (not surprisingly, given their lack of both experience and training), though she at least made some friends among the Dissenting intellectuals who lived in the area. Fanny soon married and accompanied her husband to Portugal; in 1785, when Fanny was about to have a baby, Wollstonecraft went to Lisbon, but was heartbroken when her friend died in childbirth. In 1786, she was briefly employed as governess (still without any training whatsoever) by the aristocratic Kingsborough family in Ireland; detesting her employers and critical of their lifestyle, she was bitter and miserable. She then came home to nurse her sister, who had broken down after childbirth.

She was in her early 30s when she was rescued from paralysing depression by Joseph Johnson, the radical publisher, who offered her work on his new *Analytical Review*. She began regularly reviewing and translating for him; she clearly educated herself by reading and writing. Moreover, the work, and her friendship with the radical intellectuals she met through Johnson, built up her confidence as a writer. He published her first book, *Thoughts on the Education of Daughters*, in 1787; it is a well-argued plea for girls to be given the chance to develop their God-given intelligence. But it derives real power from an undercurrent of personal feeling, a sharpness and urgency that clearly sprang from Wollstonecraft's own difficulties in picking up an education as and how she could, as well as from her contempt for the frivolity of so many fashionable women. It was soon followed by *Mary, A Fiction*, which, for all its sketchiness, remains an interesting account of growing up in a society that offers girls little support and few prospects. (The titles of both her novels, *Mary, A Fiction* and the late, unfinished *Maria; Or the Wrongs of Women*, surely hint that the stories are directly rooted in her own experience.) Mary, who is intelligent and full of 'sensibility', struggles towards fulfilment in a society that offers her few opportunities. Wollstonecraft acknowledges – and begins to explore – some intriguing emotional paradoxes. Her heroine protests bitterly against masculine dominance and violence, but still dreams of protective fatherly love; she both pities her victimized mother and is full of resentment. The older woman is portrayed as indolent, wasting her time reading sentimental novels and dwelling on the love scenes. In the end, after a series of losses, Mary decides to live for others, becoming a dutiful 'feminine' woman, whose life, sadly, is an echo of her mother's. Wollstonecraft may have lacked the skill to develop her characters fully, and the book was not widely reviewed; but it remains an intriguing and revealing attempt to explore some of the dilemmas with which she herself was confronted.

By 1790, Wollstonecraft was feeling confident enough to tackle politics; *A Vindication of the Rights of Man* is a scathing – and occasionally unpleasantly personal – attack on Edmund Burke's conservative *Reflections Upon the Revolution in France*. She accuses him of sentimentality, and, indeed, a kind of corrupt femininity; she compares him to a 'celebrated beauty' desperate for admiration; he is a fantasist, not a serious thinker. Her great feminist polemic, *A Vindication of the Rights of Woman*, followed in 1792; she sets out to speak 'for my sex, not for myself', though she admits that 'most of the struggles of an eventful life have been occasioned by the oppressed state of my sex'. She takes the simple but crucial step of extending the rights of *man*, which had been asserted during the French Revolution, to *woman*.

> If the abstract rights of man will bear discussion and explanation, those of women, by a parity of reasoning, will not shrink from the same test . . . Who made man the exclusive judge, if women partake with him of the gift of reason?

Wollstonecraft admitted that, in the times in which she lived, women *were* inferior; oppressed from birth, uneducated, and insulated from the real world, most women, inevitably, grew up ignorant and lazy.

> Taught from their infancy that beauty is a woman's sceptre, the mind shapes itself to the body and roaming round its gilt cage, only seeks to adore its prison.

Masculine gallantry and flattery are seen simply as attempts to keep women in their places, and the most 'feminine' woman is the one who best fulfils male fantasies. Femininity, she argues, is too often an artificial, class-based construct, no more than an anxious

Olympe de Gouges

In 1791, in revolutionary France, Olympe de Gouges issued a *Declaration of the Rights of Woman and the Female Citizen*, arguing, clearly and forcefully, that woman is born free, and equal to man. In de Gouges' account, in the old days, a woman who was beautiful and amiable would be offered a hundred fortunes, but she was little more than a slave. Now that she has, at least in theory, rights to liberty, property, and security, and the right to resist oppression, she must be free to mount the rostrum and speak – just as, on occasion, she has had to mount the scaffold. Like man, she is subject to the law, and may be accused and tried according to the law. But that means that woman must also be granted an equal responsibility for public life and in decisions about law and taxation; as well as the right to insist that a man recognizes his own children. In the past, both married and unmarried women have been disadvantaged, and survived by exploiting their charm. In future, de Gouges insisted, they must be free to share all man's activities. More practically, she spells out a detailed 'social contract' that would protect any woman – and any man – who chose to unite their lives.

demonstration of gentility, or would-be gentility. Girls *learn* how to be women when they are hardly more than babies; as they grow older, and in the absence of any alternative, they exploit this femininity. This, she argues, is a covert admission of women's inferiority; but women are no more 'naturally' inferior than the poor are 'naturally' stupid or ignorant. Moreover, she added, all the women she knew who had acted like rational creatures, or shown any vigour of intellect, had accidentally been allowed to run wild as children. She not only argued forcefully for better education for girls, but for something new in her day: *universal* education, at least to the age of 9.

Any woman who tries to act like a human being, Wollstonecraft remarks, risks being labelled 'masculine', and she admits that the fear of being thought unwomanly runs very deep in her sex. But if 'masculinity' means behaving rationally and virtuously, she recommends that we all 'grow more and more masculine'. Even though she defends women's *potential* powers – their capacity for all kinds of intellectual activity – she was scathing about the *actual* behaviour of many of her contemporaries. 'Told from their infancy and taught by the examples of their mothers' that they must find a man to support them, they learn to exploit their charms and looks until they find a man willing to support them. They rarely think – and have few genuine feelings. But Wollstonecraft also accepted that, though better education for women is all-important, it cannot change everything: 'Men and women must be educated in a great degree, by the opinions and manners of the society they live in.' And without a radical change in society, there can be no real 'revolution in female manners'. In this present state of things, she finds it hardly surprising that so many women are ignorant, lazy, and irresponsible.

It is interesting, and rather sad, that other women – even some highly literate ones – were among Wollstonecraft's sharpest critics. Hannah More, for example, refused even to read Wollstonecraft's book because its very title was 'absurd'; while Hannah Cowley protested coyly that 'politics are *unfeminine*'.

Wollstonecraft's *Vindication* may seem, at first glance, dated. But she is an effective writer; her prose is down-to-earth, lively, and often tart. The book is still highly readable, and it remains one of the foundation stones of contemporary feminism. Her argument is circular and, because it is exploratory, often breaking new ground, can seem at times confused. She was sharply, sometimes bitterly, aware of the personal difficulties that women experienced in her society. She argued, for example, that an understanding of childhood is central to any self-knowledge. The ability to recognize one's own childishness is crucial to maturity: 'till I can form some idea of the whole of my existence, I must be content to weep and dance like a child – long for a toy, and be tired of it as soon as I get it'. A few months later, she wrote sadly to the philosopher and novelist William Godwin that 'my imagination is forever betraying me into fresh misery, and I perceive that I shall be a child to the end of the chapter'.

As we have seen, Wollstonecraft's story *Mary, A Fiction*, based in part on her own childhood and her difficult relationship with her parents, is an intriguing attempt to explore the way women grow up. (It is also an occasionally heavy-handed celebration of her heroine's *sensibility*, that capacity for true feeling that sets her apart from other people.) The book draws on Wollstonecraft's painful recognition of the way unresolved feelings from childhood so often dominate, and even pervert, adult relationships; how, throughout our lives, we may be unknowingly re-enacting dramas rooted in the past. Women, she argued in the *Vindication*, are given little encouragement to become truly adult; they are 'made women of when they are mere children, and brought back to childhood when they ought to leave the go-cart forever'. But any girl 'whose spirits have not been damped by inactivity, or innocence by false shame, will always be a romp, and the doll will never excite attention unless confinement allows her no alternative'.

In *Thoughts on Education*, she had insisted that marriage should be based on friendship and respect rather than love; in the *Vindication* she claimed, dismissively, that most women remain obsessed by love, dreaming of happiness with some ideal and truly loving man, simply because their lives are so empty. But it is in part Wollstonecraft's inconsistencies, her implicit recognition that there are no easy solutions to the problems she explores, that make her such an enduringly interesting writer. She sadly acknowledges that even the most sensible people are likely to fall prey to 'violent and

3. Mary Wollstonecraft was one of the first English women to write
eloquently, and at times angrily, about the rights of women – and the
wrongs they often experience. Her writings have never really gone out
of fashion, and a great many modern women have responded eagerly,
and gratefully, to her work.

constant passion'; as she found, to her cost, when, on a visit to Paris in 1793, she met and fell in love with the American adventurer Gilbert Imlay. Her letters, after a happy beginning, become increasingly desperate as she complains about his blatant indifference. Pregnant by Imlay and thoroughly miserable, she still managed to work hard on her *Historical View of the Origin and Progress of the French Revolution*. Her attitude to women revolutionaries was ambiguous, to say the least, and affected, perhaps, by her anxiety, given her personal situation, to assert her own respectability. When, in October 1789, Paris marketwomen marched to Versailles and invaded the palace to put their complaints to the king, Wollstonecraft had no sympathy at all. She remarked, shuddering, that they were 'the lowest refuse of the streets, women who had thrown off the virtues of one sex without having the power to assume more than the vices of the other'.

After her baby, Fanny, was born, she undertook a trip to Sweden (taking along the baby and a nurse) on business for Imlay. Her *Letters* from the trip, published in 1796, are (unlike her letters from Paris) both perceptive and engaging. But when she arrived back in London, she found Imlay living with another woman. She survived a suicide attempt – having thrown herself into the Thames – and eventually married William Godwin.

The unfinished second novel that Wollstonecraft left behind when she died in 1797, *Maria; Or the Wrongs of Women*, is pure melodrama; but perhaps *only* melodramatic exaggeration could help her express her lasting sense of anger and frustration about the situation of women. Her heroine, Maria, has been imprisoned in a madhouse by her vicious and dishonest husband, who wants to gain control of her property. 'Was not the world a vast prison, and women born slaves?' she asks.

Perhaps the most interesting section of the book has Maria making friends with her warder, a woman called Jemima, whose story, she discovers, is at least as sad as her own. As a child she was victimized

Fiction

Through the 18th century, increasing numbers of women had been reading prose fiction because it reflected, or commented on, their own hopes and difficulties. But they were also *writing* novels that often explored the possibilities and problems in their own lives. Some concentrated on everyday domestic life; the best of them – Fanny Burney, at times, certainly Jane Austen – ask serious questions about the choices facing girls, particularly about marriage and its consequences.

'Gothic' fiction, which tackled the same questions through melodrama, was immensely popular. In scores of stories, an innocently virtuous heroine finds herself in a nightmarish world where she has to fight masculine predators for her chastity, even her survival. The 'sensibility' that characterized Samuel Richardson's heroines – Pamela (1741), who gets her man, and the tragic Clarissa (1748) – is taken to extremes, while Ann Radcliffe's *The Mysteries of Udolpho* (1794) and *The Italian* (1797) are slightly later, more knowing, versions of Wollstonecraft's *The Wrongs of Woman*. Jane Austen affectionately parodied Gothic excesses in *Northanger Abbey* (1818); but though her naïve heroine's fantasies are discounted, she is confronted with something worse: real selfishness and cruelty. The extravagances of Gothic fiction offered women readers and writers a way of exploring their feelings, of facing their darker fantasies and fears about men, marriage, and their own choices in life.

by the classic cruel stepmother, then put out to work as an apprentice, only to be raped and impregnated by her master. After aborting her baby, Jemima became a pick-pocket, was seduced and abandoned, and began working in a 'house of ill fame'. She seeks refuge in a work-house, and is then hired by the owner of a madhouse who, it turns out, preys on the inhabitants. For all its Gothic exaggerations, the novel makes a radical point: that both a middle-class and a working-class woman may find themselves helplessly exploited in a male-dominated world.

Wollstonecraft had defended her last novel angrily against criticisms from a male friend:

> I am vexed and surprised at your not thinking the situation of Maria sufficiently important, and can only account for this want of – shall I say it? Delicacy of feeling – by recollecting that you are a man.

Her point was a serious one, and one that constitutes her legacy: women must speak out, tell their own life stories, articulate their feelings, acknowledge both their own hopes and their sense of being cheated and wronged.

Wollstonecraft left notes outlining the bleakest of futures for her heroine: 'Divorced by her husband – Her lover unfaithful – Pregnancy – Miscarriage – Suicide.' She probably could never have imagined a convincingly happy ending for her. Though Wollstonecraft herself, all too briefly, found peace and contentment with William Godwin, she died a few months after they married, giving birth to her second child: another Mary, who would grow up to marry the poet Percy Shelley, and to write that extraordinary and troubling novel, *Frankenstein*.

Chapter 4
The early 19th century: reforming women

The 19th century saw an increasingly widespread and articulate statement of women's claims – perhaps in reaction to the emergence of an image of true 'femininity' that seemed to become more constricted as the century wore on: a class-based ideal of gentility and refinement. But though many women (and men) spoke out eloquently against and acted on their beliefs, it was not until the second half of the century that any organized campaigns – particularly for better education for women, for the possibility of their working outside the home, for a reform in the laws affecting married women, and for the right to vote – began to emerge.

In 1843, a married woman, Marion Reid, had published in Edinburgh *A Plea for Women*, which has been described, rightly, as the most thorough and effective statement by a woman since Mary Wollstonecraft's *Vindication*. Reid covered most of the areas that would preoccupy reformers for the rest of the century and her book deserves to be better known. (At the time, it was widely read, and reprinted several times, though it seems to have been more popular in America than in England.) Reid offers a cool and damning analysis of the way her contemporaries – and, she admits, they are mainly other women – talk so confidently about a 'woman's sphere', and equate womanliness with the renunciation of self. 'Womanly' behaviour, in practice, means 'good humour and attention to her husband, keeping her children neat and clean, and attending to domestic arrangements'. But Reid insists, more forcibly than anyone else in the period, that this apparently noble and virtuous 'self-renunciation' in practice usually involves 'a most criminal self-extinction'.

The education that most girls are given merely 'cramps and confines' them, she claims: 'Any symptom of independent thought is quickly repressed . . . the majority of girls are subdued into mere automatons.' Reid also comments bitterly on the almost insurmountable difficulties many women face in 'obtaining the means of a good substantial education'. Most girls are brought up to 'a mechanical performance of duty . . . their own minds all the while lying barren and unfruitful'. This question of education would remain crucially important all through the 19th century; too little seemed to have changed since the days of Mary Astell and Mary Wollstonecraft. Education for girls – whether at home by governesses, who were often barely trained, or at inadequate schools – remained a hit and miss affair.

Reid is careful to acknowledge women's domestic responsibilities, though she claims that most women go about their household duties in 'a cold, hard, mechanical, loveless spiritless way'. She admits that, as things are, domestic work must form part, and 'perhaps even the chief part', of a woman's life. But she argues that there is no reason why woman should be *limited* to domesticity. A shade reluctantly, she allows that some 'subordination' of herself may be 'due to man'. But, she asks, 'if woman's rights are not the same as those of man, what are they?' In one sense, she admits, 'woman was made for man, yet in another and higher she was also made for herself'. Innocence, she argues, is not the same thing as virtue.

But a married woman – living in a 'shackled condition' – has no rights over her own property; even the produce of her own labour is at the disposal of her husband, who can, if he chooses, take and 'waste it in dissipation and excess'. Moreover, 'her children, as well as her fortune, are the property of her husband'.

In what was, for the times, her most radical argument, Reid asserts that 'womanliness' is quite compatible with voting. After all, woman, as much as man, is 'a rational, moral and accountable creature'. She has no particular wish to see women representatives, she remarks cautiously; probably few women would 'consent to be chosen' and few electors would choose them. But she sees no reason why women should not stand, if any are 'able or willing to overleap natural barriers'.

The two best-known 19th-century arguments for women's rights were written by men; though in both cases, the authors – William Thompson and John Stuart Mill – acknowledge the influence and inspiration of their wives. It is intriguing that neither of these women – who were well educated and articulate – chose to speak out for themselves. Was this a nervousness about breaking with convention and speaking out in their own voices, or simply a tactical recognition that a man's arguments might be taken more seriously?

In 1825 the Irish-born William Thompson published his *Appeal of One Half of the Human Race, Women, against the Pretensions of the Other Half, Men, to Restrain them in Political and thence in Civil and Domestic Slavery*. He describes the book as 'the protest of at least one man and one woman' against the 'degradation of one half of the adult portion of the human race'. It is addressed to, and acknowledges the inspiration of, the widowed Anna Wheeler. Anna Wheeler had been married off when she was only 15 years of age; the couple had six children, but when her husband proved a drunkard, Anna found the courage to leave him, and in 1818 spent some time in France, where she came into contact with Saint Simonian socialists. After her husband's death two years later, she returned to London, where she became well known for her interest in reform movements. She was attacked by no less a figure than Benjamin Disraeli, who remarked sarcastically that Anna was 'something between Jeremy Bentham and Meg Merrilees, very clever but awfully revolutionary'.

Thompson shared and expressed Anna Wheeler's radical views. 'I hear you indignantly reject the boon of equality with such creatures as men now are', he wrote to her: 'With you I would equally elevate both sexes.' The book concentrates on the situation of the married woman, who is reduced to being a piece of 'movable property and an ever-obedient servant to the bidding of man'. For a married woman, her home becomes a 'prison-house'. The house itself, as well as everything in it, belongs to the husband, 'and of all fixtures the most abject is his breeding machine, the wife'. Married women are in fact slaves, their situation no better than that 'of Negroes in the West Indies'. Mothers are denied rights over their children and over family property, and most are treated like 'any other upper servant'.

The *Appeal* was in part couched as an answer to James Mill's *Essay on Government*, well known at the time, which argued that women need no political rights as they are adequately represented by their fathers or husbands. 'What happens to women who have neither husband nor father?' Thompson asks. He then goes on to attack, pungently and at length, the unthinking assumption that the interests of husband and wife are always identical, and to criticize, bitterly, the unjust situation. He also looks forward to a time when the children of all classes, both girls and boys, will be equally provided for and educated.

Anna Wheeler later went on to become an effective writer and lecturer on women's rights. Sadly, her own daughter strongly disapproved of her radical inclinations, claiming that she was

> unfortunately deeply imbued with the pernicious fallacies of the French Revolution, which had then more or less seared their trace through Europe, and ... was besides strongly tainted by the corresponding poison of Mrs Wollstonecraft's book.

Interestingly, William Thompson, too, criticizes Mary Wollstonecraft, but for quite opposite reasons: he attacked her 'narrow views' and the 'timidity and impotence of her conclusions'. (He was perhaps betraying his own lack of historical awareness.) But he calls on women to make their own demands for education, and for civil and political rights; in the long run, he feels, that must benefit men as well:

> As your bondage has chained down man to the ignorance and vices of despotism, so will your liberation reward him with knowledge, with freedom and happiness.

In 1869 John Stuart Mill published *The Subjection of Women*, which also argued that the subordination of women was both wrong and 'one of the chief hindrances to human improvement'. (Ironically, he was the son of the James Mill whose conservative views on women had so infuriated William Thompson.) Mill was profoundly influenced by Harriet Taylor, whom he had met in 1830. She was already married, with two small sons; the pair maintained an intense friendship for nearly twenty years, and eventually, two years after her husband died in 1851, they were able to marry. Harriet had published a short article on 'The Enfranchisement of Women' in the *Westminster Review* in 1851; and she had written, though, interestingly, not published, papers that criticized the marriage laws and claimed a woman's rights and responsibilities towards her own children. When she and Mill eventually married, he remarked that he felt it his duty to make 'a formal protest against the existing law of marriage' on the grounds that it gave the man 'legal power over the person, property and freedom of action of the other party, independent of her own wishes and will'. Mill admitted that

> the opinion was in my mind little more than an abstract principle ... that perception of the vast practical bearings of women's disabilities which found expression in the book on *The Subjection of Women* was acquired mainly through her [Harriet's] teaching.

19th-century American feminism

In the 19th-century United States, feminism emerged out of the anti-slavery movement, in which women were very active. Anti-slavery societies proliferated from the 1830s onward; ironically, some groups were open only to whites. In London in 1840 a World Convention on slavery was attended by Americans, including Elizabeth Cady Stanton; women were banned from taking part in the debate. That moved Stanton and Lucretia Mott to become feminists. In 1848, they organized a women's convention in Seneca Falls, New York, and campaigned for rights, including the vote, for women and for blacks. Sarah and Angelina Grimke, from a Southern slaveholding family, but converted Quakers, became ardent and effective abolitionists. In 1863, Angelina published *An Appeal to the Christian Women of the Southern States*, and two years later, *Letters on the Equality of the Sexes*. She responded angrily to criticism that she had stepped outside woman's proper sphere. A former slave, Sojourner Truth, mocked clerics who insisted that women needed to be protected by men, and spoke out angrily after the Civil War and the emancipation of slaves, when the vote was given to former slaves – but only males. In 1920, women were enfranchised, but it was only in 1970 that the vote was given to all blacks.

Mill based his arguments in the *Subjection* on the belief that the then existing – and blatantly unequal – relationship between the sexes was anything but natural. 'Was there ever any domination which did not appear natural to those who possessed it?' he asks, citing the way, until recently, its beneficiaries had defended the slave trade in America. What we presently call womanliness is something artificial, 'the result of forced repression in some directions, unnatural stimulations in others'. He seems to have come to this notion only gradually, and probably under Harriet's influence; in 1832, not long after they met, he had written informing her that 'the great occupation of woman should be to *beautify* life . . . to diffuse beauty, elegance, & grace everywhere'.

But in the *Subjection* he denies that

> anyone knows, or can know, the nature of the two sexes as long as they have only been seen in their present relation to one another. All the moralities tell them that it is the duty of woman, and all the current sentimentalities that it is their nature, to live for others.

It is hardly surprising, given the poverty of their education and the narrowness of their lives, he argues, that women have not yet produced 'great and luminous ideas'. He also claims, even more dubiously, that they have not yet created 'a literature of their own'. Ann Radcliffe, Fanny Burney, Jane Austen, Susan Ferrier, the Brontë sisters: they all seem to have escaped his notice.

In an ideal world, Mill believed, men and women would resemble each other: men would be more unselfish, and women would be free of the 'exaggerated self-abnegation' expected of them. Mill never goes so far as to argue for the possibility of divorce. But he insists that there is no justification for not giving women the vote immediately, and under exactly the same conditions as men; in fact, he remarked, many of them deserve it more than some of the present voters. In 1866, Mill presented the first women's petition for the vote, and he moved amendments to the 1867 Reform Bill in favour of women.

Some modern feminists have criticized Mill for concentrating almost exclusively on married women, while ignoring the situation of, say, daughters or single women. But married women – as both

Reid and Thompson had recognized earlier – were indeed, legally at least, particularly vulnerable. The problems wives might face were dramatically illustrated in the notorious case of Caroline Norton. Born in 1808, she was the granddaughter of the playwright Richard Sheridan, and she was beautiful, lively, and well educated. She certainly never set out to become a champion of women's rights, asserting, in fact, that she 'never pretended to the wild and ridiculous doctrine of equality'. She married, she once admitted, partly because she 'particularly dreaded' the prospect of 'living and dying an old maid'. But she found herself, in 1826, tied to a husband who soon proved hopelessly uncongenial. Their relationship gradually deteriorated, and broke down in scenes of outright violence. Eventually, Norton not only refused his wife access to her own property (everything she had inherited, and everything that she later earned); he denied her all contact with her three children. He vengefully pushed her into a harsh public spotlight, making her the focus of scandal when he (probably unjustifiably) accused her of adultery with the then Prime Minister, Lord Melbourne. Though the case was dismissed, Caroline Norton understandably felt humiliated and betrayed, and her reputation was permanently tarnished.

Norton could not go to law to defend or protect herself, or to argue her rights of access to her own children, because, she discovered, a married woman had no legal existence. 'It is a hard thing to feel legally so helpless and dependent while *in fact* I am as able to support myself as an intelligent man working in a modest profession', she complained. In 1838, she supported the passing of a bill reforming an Infants Custody Act which gave a mother limited rights over her children until they were 7, and in 1854 and 1855, she produced pamphlets based on her own case: *The Separation of Mother and Child by the Law of Custody of Infants Considered* and *English Laws for Women in the 19th Century*, both of which reached a wide audience. 'I have learned the law respecting married women piecemeal, but suffering every one of its defects of protection', she remarked. In her 1855 *Letter to the Queen* supporting a proposed bill on the Reform of Marriage and Divorce, she wrote that 'I believe in my obscurer position that I am permitted to be the example on which a particular law shall be reformed'. A Divorce Reform Act was passed in 1857, but the circumstances in which a woman could file for divorce remained very limited.

Though Norton's life dramatically illustrated some of the cruel anomalies in the status of married women, hers was certainly not a solitary, or even an unusual, case. Charlotte Brontë, for example, when she married not long before she died, discovered that her husband owned the copyright to her novels, as well as everything she earned. But Caroline Norton dissociated herself from other women who, in the mid-1850s were beginning to meet together over women's issues, and who soon took up the cause that her case had publicized; indeed, a Married Women's Property Committee, set up by the group known as 'the Ladies of Langham Place', was probably the first organized feminist group in England. But Caroline Norton, perhaps feeling that she had been too much in the public eye, perhaps anxious to retain at least the shreds of her reputation, kept her distance.

Florence Nightingale was another remarkable woman who flatly refused to be associated with the emerging women's movement, though, in the long run, her example proved inspiring, and much more effective than anything she actually said. She famously remarked that 'I am brutally indifferent to the wrongs or the rights of my sex', and insisted that if women are unemployed 'it is because they won't work'. She would be prepared to pay a woman well to act as her secretary, she once said, but could find no one who was either able or willing to take on the work. But she herself came up sharply against the way society divided the sexes and constricted women's lives. The daughter of a well-off and well-connected family, she complained that she was a martyr to genteel and leisured femininity. Why, she asked sarcastically, would it be 'more ridiculous for a man than a woman to do worsted work and drive out everyday in a carriage?' 'Why should we laugh if we were to see a parcel of men sitting around a drawing-room table in the morning and think it all right if they were women?'

Nightingale seems to developed her interest in nursing after undertaking some typically female duties – looking after her grandmother and her old nurse. But her growing interest in the work led to vocal disapproval, and to constant demands on her time from her mother and her sister Parthenope. In 1844, the family flatly refused to let her spend time at Salisbury Infirmary. 'There is nothing like the tyranny of a good English family', Nightingale once remarked bitterly, claiming that most women 'have no God, no country, no duty to them at all except family'. But in 1849 she managed a visit to Kaiserwerth in Germany, an orphan asylum and hospital run by Lutheran deaconesses. Though she was critical of its standard of nursing and hygiene, she admitted that 'I find the deepest interest in everything here and am so well in body and mind'. But at the age of 37, she was still asking bitterly, in a fragment of a novel which she called *Cassandra*, 'Why have women passion, intellect, moral activity – these three – and a place in society where no one of the three can be exercised?'

Her life changed when, in 1853, her father decided, against his wife's strongly expressed wishes, to allow Florence £500 a year. She was finally freed from domestic tyranny, and in August of that year, she became resident superintendent of the Invalid Gentlewoman's Institution in Harley Street. She had already determinedly set about learning everything she could about nursing, and regularly rose at dawn to study Government Blue Books, though she was still occasionally plagued by worries about whether it was 'unsuitable and unbecoming' for a woman to devote herself to 'works of charity in hospitals and elsewhere'. In 1854 she worked at the Middlesex Hospital in London during an outbreak of cholera.

Nightingale had established enough of a reputation to be invited to go to Scutari with a group of nurses during the Crimean War; she soon became a national heroine. Ironically, at the time she was hailed,

4. Florence Nightingale was a national heroine – the 'Lady with the Lamp' – often, as here, celebrated for her compassion and womanly tenderness towards the wounded soldiers in the Crimea, rather than for her truly remarkable talent for administration and organization.

sentimentally, as a truly 'feminine' woman – indeed, a ministering angel – who had renounced a life of luxury and high fashion to bring comfort to wounded soldiers in the Crimea. Images of the 'Lady with the Lamp' were widely circulated, icons that celebrated her compassion, but also her delicate refinement, her gentility, and her ladylike grace. Nightingale certainly had great concern for her patients and sympathy with the ordinary soldier. But her greatest contribution, perhaps, lay in the fact that she was such a superbly efficient and clear-headed administrator. 'I am now clothing the British army', she wrote at the time, 'I am really cook, housekeeper, scavenger . . . washerwoman, general dealer, storekeeper.' The years during and following the Crimean War were undoubtedly the most satisfying, in every way the happiest, period of her life.

For she refused to stop when the war ended, instead undertaking an ambitious investigation into the health of the British Army. When, later in her life, she retired to bed for long periods – a habit that made a parody of fashionably 'feminine' fragility – it was simply in order to have time to work more effectively, undisturbed by the demands of her mother and sister. She remains an intriguing paradox: on the surface, and by reputation, the archetype of 'feminine' self-sacrifice and devotion to others; in fact, a model of determined, even heroic, self-assertion, who opened up the possibilities available to women. Her example certainly helped to make acceptable the idea of a woman training for some specific occupation, and working outside the home or the family business.

Harriet Martineau, too, insisted that her defence of women was impersonal and rational. Martineau, who dismissed Mary Wollstonecraft as actually harmful to the cause of women, saw herself as an educator. Her first book, *Illustrations of Political Economy*, appeared in 1832 when she was 30, an unknown provincial. It did well, and she became a widely read journalist who specialized in popularizing economic and social theory. Having travelled in the United States and worked there with Abolitionists, Martineau applied their arguments about slaves to women:

justice is denied on no better plea than the right of the strongest. In both cases the acquiescence of the many and the burning discontent of the few of the oppressed, testify, the one to the actual degradation of the class, and the other to its fitness for the enjoyment of human rights.

At the same time, she consistently, and perhaps short-sightedly, refused to support 'the cause of women', arguing that 'women, like men, must obtain whatever they show themselves fit for'. After *Society in America* was published, dozens of women wrote to her complaining of how the 'law and custom' of England oppressed them and asked for help in changing things; others offered 'money, effort, courage in enduring obloquy' if she would offer advice.

But throughout, Martineau nervously shied away from overt emotion. She was deeply unsympathetic to a woman like Caroline Norton, whose exposure of her personal problems in an attempt to change marriage laws, Martineau felt, 'violates all decency'. However, unexpectedly and touchingly, some of her surviving letters to her mother suggest real anxiety about her own choice of an independent life.

> I fully expect that both you and I shall occasionally feel as if I did not discharge a daughter's duty, but we shall both remind ourselves that I am now as much a citizen of the world as any professional *son* of yours could be. My hours of solitary work and of visiting will leave you much to yourself.

Understandably, perhaps, she never fully came to terms with this conflict between her own ambition and the current ideal of proper feminine behaviour. When she was 35, Martineau was offered the editorship of a new economics periodical, which would have meant money, prestige, and have been the culmination of her own ambitions, and of her hopes for women. She dithered, until a disapproving letter arrived from her brother James, and – obviously half-relieved – she turned the opportunity down. Instead, she wrote an intriguing novel, *Deerbrook*, which indirectly explores, not just her own fears, hopes, indecisions, but the doubts and problems that still plagued so many of her female contemporaries. She died in 1876.

By the middle years of the 19th century, a whole series of women were working quietly but impressively for specific reforms, and in the process opening up new areas to other women. Frances Power Cobbe, for example, bitterly recalled the expensive boarding school which she had attended in Brighton: it was, she claimed, totally inadequate. The pupils were crowded round tables in a single room with a 'hideous clatter'; a piano would be pounding upstairs, and down below a roomful of girls reading and reciting their lessons to governesses. Her own experience, she came to realize, was typical. Girls' education was in urgent need of improvement; schools in her grandmother's day, she speculated, had probably been better than contemporary ones. Despite her unpromising educational start, Cobbe went on to write vividly and thoughtfully, not just about education, but about other difficulties faced by both single and married women.

She was eloquent, for example, about the situation of wives trapped in miserable marriages. 'We are used', she wrote, 'to tales of drunken ruffians, stumbling home from the gin-houses' who assault their miserable wives. But 'who could have imagined it possible that well-born and well-educated men, in honourable professions, should be guilty of the same brutality?' She occasionally lapsed into conventional sentimentality:

> we want [woman's] sense of the law of love to complete man's sense of the law of justice; we want her influence inspiring virtue by gentle promptings within, to complete man's external legislation of morality . . . We want her genius for detail, her tenderness for age and suffering, her comprehension of the wants of childhood . . . .

But as a well-regarded journalist, she backed the idea of university education for women and campaigned quietly for a Married Women's Property Act. But she always insisted, rather too emphatically to be credible, that her feminism was nothing personal: 'If I have become in mature years a "Woman's Rights woman" it is not because in my own person I have been made to feel a woman's wrongs.'

Marriage in the novel

Marriage remained a central and engrossing theme for 19th-century novelists, but relations between husbands and wives were rarely seen as particularly fulfilling. In Charlotte Brontë's *Jane Eyre* (1847), the heroine's love affair with Mr Rochester is a more sophisticated, and haunting, version of Gothic melodrama, though she is allowed a happier ending – once Rochester has been left crippled and helpless. Mrs Gaskell's heroines all want, however vaguely, something more than convention allows them. Mary Ann Evans – who, interestingly, wrote as George Eliot – explores the often difficult relations between brother and sister in *The Mill on the Floss* (1860). In *Middlemarch* (1871–2), the intelligent, idealistic Dorothea, seeking to devote her life to something – or someone – worthy, is soon trapped in a miserable marriage. Though she finally achieves happiness of a kind with another man, she feels that there was something better that she might have done. George Meredith's *The Egoist* (1871) is a chilling study of a marriage in which the woman is simply a status symbol; his *Diana of the Crossways* (1885) offers a troubling fictional version of Caroline Norton's disastrous marriage. George Gissing's *The Odd Women* (1893) is a sympathetic account of spinsters caring for an orphaned baby who, they hope, will grow up to become 'a brave woman'.

Chapter 5
The late 19th century: campaigning women

It was not until the second half of the 19th century that anything like a true women's 'movement' began to emerge in England. This movement converged particularly around Barbara Leigh Smith and the group of friends who had become known – after one of their early meeting places – as 'the Ladies of Langham Place'. The group initiated more organized campaigns around issues that had already been clearly defined: women's urgent need for better education and for increased possibilities of employment, as well as the improvement of the legal position of married women.

The women came together, in part, as a reaction against what seemed to be a narrowing definition of 'femininity' and an increasingly conventional and constricting notion of a proper 'womanly sphere'. A Victorian woman's highest virtue seems to have been nervously, if frequently, equated with genteel passivity. A middle-class woman who had to earn her own living might be lucky enough to find a poorly paid position as a governess, even though she had probably been skimpily educated herself. Few other occupations were open to her. And there was still no way out for a woman who found herself unhappily married.

Sadly, even women with impressive achievements of their own, women who had written with great sympathy and insight about women's lives and struggles, seem sometimes to have shied away from an emerging feminism. Mary Ann Evans – George Eliot – despite her remarkable understanding in *Middlemarch* (1871–2) of the way a woman's intelligence and talents may be denied an adequate outlet, and despite the fact that she became a close friend and supporter of Barbara Leigh Smith, remarked in 1853 that 'woman does not yet deserve a better lot than man gives her'. And she praised the way an 'exquisite type of gentleness, tenderness, possible maternity' may suffuse 'a woman's being with affectionateness'. In 1856, the novelist Mrs Gaskell, author of *Ruth* (1853) and *North and South* (1855), dismissed the very notion of women training as doctors:

> I would not trust a mouse to a woman if a man's judgement was to be had. Women have no judgement. They've tact and sensitiveness, genius and hundreds of fine and loving qualities; but are at best angelic geese as to matters requiring serious and long medical education.

And in 1857 Elizabeth Barrett Browning argued in *Aurora Leigh* that:

> A woman . . . must prove what she can do
> Before she does it, prate of women's rights,
> Of woman's mission, woman's function till
> The men (who are prating too on their side) cry
> A woman's function plainly is . . . to talk.

Barbara Leigh Smith (after she married, she broke with convention and simply added her husband's name, Bodichon, to her own) was born into a family that was wealthy but untypical: her parents were not married. Her father had always encouraged her to read, and made her a generous allowance, which meant she could afford to travel widely. She spent time in Europe with Bessie Rayner Parkes, who went on to write *Remarks on the Education of Girls*, and who also insisted that single women would prove crucial to any improvement in the lot of all women. (A review at the time mocked both Parkes and Leigh Smith, who had just published a pamphlet on *Women and Work*, sneering that 'women are fatally deficient in the power of close consecutive thought'.)

In 1857, recuperating in Algeria after an illness, Leigh Smith met the man would become her husband, the physician Eugene Bodichon. They spent a year in America after their wedding, where, in Boston, New York, and New Orleans, she met women who were interested in education, as well as others who had trained as doctors. At Seneca Falls she had long conversations with Lucretia Mott, who was an activist both in the anti-slavery movement and in the emerging campaign for women's rights. Leigh Smith would go on to work on the areas which seemed most urgent: the legal problems of married women, the urgent necessity for better education and training for women, as well as the need to extend the limited employment possibilities available to them.

In 1854, Barbara Leigh Smith had produced a pamphlet titled *A Brief Summary in Plain Language of the Most Important Laws of England Concerning Women*. She began by considering the contradictions limiting single women: they were allowed to vote at parish, but not, even if they were tax-paying property owners, at parliamentary elections. She moved on to the even greater disabilities facing married women: 'a man and his wife are one person in law; the wife loses all her rights as a single woman, and her existence is entirely absorbed to that of her husband'. She discussed the question of marriage settlements, and the custody of children if parents separated; and even uncovered the curious and troubling legal fact that, once a couple were formally engaged, a woman could not dispose of her property without her fiancé's knowledge and agreement. Her manifesto sold for a few pence; it was very widely read, and went to three editions. In December of the following year, she and a group of like-minded women – including Bessie Parkes and Anna Jameson – formed a Married Women's Property Committee (England's first organized feminist group), which circulated petitions for law reform throughout the country, and had soon had gathered some 2,400 signatures. The Committee's intervention led to a series of amendments which alleviated the financial situation of married women, even if the changes still did not radically redefine their rights.

Leigh Smith had also produced an article, first published in the newly founded *English Women's Journal* in 1858, in which she argued strongly against the view that middle-class women, because they were expected to marry, should be prepared for nothing else. Large numbers would probably never marry, and might have to support themselves; but even those who did marry, she argued, should be equipped to educate their children, and, if necessary, to take on work outside the home. Moreover, she insisted on the value of work for its own sake.

> To bring a family of 12 children into the world is not itself a noble vocation . . . To be a noble woman is better than being a mother to a noble man.

She even invoked Queen Victoria, who was, after all, both a mother *and* a working monarch. At the same time, Leigh Smith insisted on greater recognition of the value of the very real work that women already did, looking after the home and raising their families. Leigh Smith actually set up a primary school in London, which survived for nearly ten years. Boys and girls were taught together; and her own nieces and the children of her friends learned alongside the children of workers who lived in the neighbourhood.

The *English Women's Journal*, which was at first largely funded by Leigh Smith, seems to have reached – and often inspired to action – a reasonably wide audience. Even George Eliot, who had initially been very doubtful, wrote at the end of 1859 reassuring her friend that it '*must* be doing good substantially – stimulating woman to useful work and rousing people generally to some consideration of women's needs'. But Leigh Smith and Bessie Parkes were soon confronted, at first hand, with the problems of women's employment. Readers of their *Journal*, desperate for work, began coming to their office, which had moved from Langham Place to Cavendish Square. They decided to keep an employment register – only to discover how few opportunities were in fact available for women. Many men bitterly resented the prospect of women entering their trades; women, they argued, would lower wages for everyone, and their presence might well force men into unemployment.

Employment possibilities concerned other women as well. Earlier that year, Harriet Martineau – who was familiar with the work of the Langham Place group, and probably influenced by it, though she was never actually a member – had published, in the *Edinburgh Review*, an article called 'Female Industry' which took a cool, hard-headed look at the few openings that were actually available to women. She saw clearly that the situation of women was changing; more and more women had no choice but to go out to work. The concept of 'earning one's bread' was, she argued, a fairly recent one for men as well as women.

> We live in a new commercial and industrial economy, but our ideas, our language and our arrangements have not altered in any corresponding degree. We go on talking as if it were still true that every woman is, or ought to be, supported by father, brother or husband.

Poor women might labour in the fields or in factories; apart from that, Martineau could see only two – equally low-paid – possibilities: needlework or teaching. Like Barbara Leigh Smith, she insisted that women's education must be extended and improved, and that a 'fair field' should be opened to their 'power and energies'.

She praised Elizabeth Blackwell, who had trained as a doctor in America, and who was visiting England at the time. (Barbara Leigh

Smith and Bessie Parkes helped to organize the talks Blackwell gave, not just in London but in provincial centres as well.) But unlike many of these early feminists, and because she believed strongly that women should make no more than moderate and rational claims, she had little sympathy with the emerging demand for the vote.

Francis Power Cobbe, as noted in the previous chapter an advocate in the campaign for the Married Women's Property Act and of education for women, did go on to campaign for women's suffrage, believing that women could not necessarily rely on men to protect them or their interests. Her arguments to this end sometimes betray a hint of class arrogance: she was angry that 'we women of the upper ranks – constitutionally qualified by the possession of property (and, I may be permitted to add, naturally qualified by education and intelligence at least up to the level of the "illiterate" order of voters) are still denied the suffrage'. She was always profoundly conservative, though her disapproval of the radical wing of the Conservative Party led her to resign from the emerging suffrage movement in 1867.

Emily Davies was another staunch conservative, in everything except her recognition that education was central to any improvement in women's lot. 'It is no wonder,' the young Davies wrote, 'that people who have not learned to do anything cannot find anything to do'. When she had to go to nurse her brother, who had fallen ill in Algiers, she had the great good fortune to meet Barbara Leigh Smith, who encouraged her, and reassured her that there were many other women who would sympathize with her longings and dissatisfactions. Back in England, Davies (along with her friend Elizabeth Garrett) visited Langham Place, which had become the headquarters of both the *English Women's Journal* and a Society for Promoting the Employment of Women. She felt inspired and, when she returned to her home in the North, formed a Northumberland and Durham branch of the Society, as well as writing a series of letters to her local paper arguing the importance of increased employment opportunities for women. She was scathing about the meagre intellectual training available to girls like herself: 'Do they go to school? No. Do they have governesses? No. They have lessons and get on as well as they can.' And she described, with great personal feeling,

> the weight of discouragement produced by being told, that as women, nothing much is ever to be expected of them ... that whatever they do they must not interest themselves, except in a second-hand and shallow way, in the pursuits of men, for in such pursuits they must always expect to fail.

Women know how this kind of attitude 'stifles and chills; how hard it is to work courageously through it'.

But Davies was also encouraged by the growing recognition among the Langham Place group that education was all-important. In London, the recently established Queen's College and Bedford College were offering something like an adequate schooling to (some) middle-class girls, and in 1862 Davies managed to form a committee to further the prospects of women taking the University Local Examinations, which had been established in 1858. It took a great deal of slow, careful organization and negotiation before Cambridge agreed, as an experiment in 1865, that women could attempt the same exams as men. Though Davies was always a realist, she never retreated from her belief that girls must be offered exactly the same education as men, at both school and university level. Her book on *The Higher Education of Women*, which appeared in 1866, is careful not to state the claims too strongly. Davies admitted that women will probably 'never do as well as men ... But that does not seem to me a reason for not doing their best and choosing for themselves what they will try.' She managed to raise money (Barbara Leigh Smith contributed generously) to found a women's higher education college, which was set up at Hitchin in Hertfordshire with, initially, just five students. In 1873, it moved to Cambridge and became Girton College; this was followed in 1879 by Lady Margaret Hall in Oxford. But for all Emily Davies's radical ideas – she insisted from the start that women students take the same exams as men – she certainly did not want women to enjoy the same freedoms as male students. She expected that her students would always behave decorously, with the utmost propriety; unconventional and 'unfeminine' behaviour might, she believed, jeopardize the whole project.

Emily Davies's pioneering work was crucially important, though, perhaps inevitably, it was a long time before women achieved anything approaching real equality in higher education. In London, Queen's and Bedford Colleges began awarding degrees to women in 1878. But Oxford women became full members of the University only in 1919, and, paradoxically, though Cambridge granted women 'titular' degrees in 1921, they were not recognized as full members of the University until 1948.

Elizabeth Garrett (later Garrett Anderson) also received support from the Langham Place group in her prolonged and courageous efforts, in the face of what now seems the most extraordinary opposition, to train as a doctor. She was often the butt of crude jokes. Some male students announced their disapproval of 'the impropriety of males and females mingling . . . while studying subjects which hitherto have been considered of a delicate nature', while the *Lancet* journal dismissed her efforts to train as 'morbid'. Nothing shook Garrett in her determination. For one thing, she believed that women doctors would be a great boon 'to many suffering women'. Moreover, the work interested her deeply, and she knew that she would be good at it.

She was encouraged by the example of Elizabeth Blackwell, who had managed to graduate in medicine at a small college in New York State in 1849, and had opened a dispensary for women and children in the New York slums. But when Blackwell visited London, she was sometimes greeted with harsh criticism: 'it is impossible that a woman whose hands reek with gore can be possessed of the same nature or feelings as the generality of women', one columnist remarked. Elizabeth Garrett had to struggle hard to convince her own mother that her patient determination to work in medicine was not wrong, or morbid, but the 'result of a healthy, active energy'. Fortunately, her father was more supportive, and Garrett herself quietly, patiently persisted. She studied midwifery in Scotland, then won her M.D. diploma in Paris. Even the *British Medical Journal*, which had been consistently hostile to the idea of women in medicine, admitted that 'everyone must admire the indomitable perseverance and pluck which Miss Garrett has shown'. By 1870, when she was persuaded to stand for election to the London School Board, she had obviously become a highly respected and popular public figure, and she received more votes than any other candidate.

One of the most important and far-reaching campaigns in the later part of the 19th century was also one of the most unexpected: the agitation against the Contagious Diseases Acts which dramatically exposed the cruel hypocrisies of the double sexual standard. The first of the Acts had been passed in 1864; in certain ports and garrison towns, police were given the authority to arrest any woman who was merely *suspected* of being a prostitute, subject her, sometimes brutally, to an internal examination, and if there were any signs of venereal disease, to confine her to hospital. There were extensions to the Act in 1866 and 1869. Women soon began protesting; they included Elizabeth Garrett, Florence Nightingale, and Harriet Martineau, who argued that 'the regulation system creates horrors worse than those which it is supposed to restrain'.

By 1869, a Ladies National Association for the Repeal of the Contagious Diseases Acts had been set up, a number of eminently respectable women forming the first real, and effective, pressure group. In the first instance, their campaign launched an attack on specific laws that bore very brutally on prostitutes or suspected prostitutes; but they soon extended the argument to dramatize the workings of the double sexual standard, with its disastrous effects on both men and women all through society. Josephine Butler soon became the group's leader. The well-educated daughter of a Liberal family, she was beautiful, devout, and eminently respectable – hence a superbly effective propagandist for what many people regarded as a highly unrespectable cause. She had already begun working with prostitutes when, after the tragic death of their only daughter, she and her husband moved to Liverpool. 'I became possessed with an irresistible desire to go forth and find some pain keener than my own', she remarked. She took some unhappy 'fallen' girls into her own home, and raised money to establish a small 'House of Rest' that would care 'for dying Magdalenes'.

Butler had already displayed a keen interest in the problems facing women. A pamphlet on *The Education and Employment of Women*, published in 1868, made the argument, familiar by then, for better education, and also – given the number of unmarried women in England – for adequate training to enable them to support themselves. In 1869, she and other sympathetic women formed a Ladies National Association; Butler made a superbly effective figurehead and leader. Her speeches and writings effectively combine cool, clear argument with passionate feeling. In a pamphlet written in 1871, and based on her own experience with prostitutes, Butler argued that the Contagious Diseases Acts amounted to a suspension of the Habeas Corpus Act. They 'virtually introduce a species of villeinage or slavery. I use the word not sentimentally but in the strictest legal sense.' The issue, and her protest, kindled the imagination and feelings of women all through the country. In an 1870 letter to the Prime Minister, a member of the Ladies National Association had insisted that

> there is not one of the mothers, wives, sisters, or daughters whom you cherish with proud affection who dare safely assert that, had she been born in the same unprotected, unfenced position, in the very jaws of poverty and vice . . . she, too, in the innocent ignorance of her unfledged girlhood, might not have slipped, like them, into that

awful gulf from which society at large has long done its best to make escape hopeless.

Josephine Butler and her rapidly growing band of highly respectable supporters soon became a remarkably effective pressure group; their campaign exposed, dramatically, a brutal double sexual standard that long custom had made virtually invisible. And, crucially, they argued it was a double standard that oppressed, not just prostitutes, but most women, in all kinds of subtle ways, that spread through almost every aspect of their everyday domestic and working lives. Later, giving evidence to a Parliamentary Select Committee, Butler pointed out the indirect but disastrous effects of the Act on men as well as women. When she had visited Chatham, 'I saw there evidence of the degradation of the young soldiers who first join the army . . . There were boys who appeared to be not more than thirteen . . . it was as solemn as hell itself.' The real villains, the real exploiters, were in her view the pimps, the people who made money by 'setting up a house in which women are sold to men'.

In the 1880s, Annie Besant tackled a different, and perhaps even more urgent, form of exploitation. Discovering the truly terrible conditions in which women worked at the Bryant and May match-making factory in East London, she sent a deeply, and effectively, emotional letter to the many shareholders who happened to be clergymen:

> let there rise before you the pale worn face of another man's daughter . . . as she pulls off her battered hat and shows a head robbed of its hair by the constant rubbing of the carried boxes, robbed thereof that your dividends might be larger, Sir Cleric . . . I hold you up to the public opprobrium you deserve . . .

Her charges were widely publicized, and aroused great public concern. The match girls led sizeable protest marches in London, and were eventually allowed to form their own union.

Progress on all these issues facing women was now underway. But women – as well as a few male champions like Thompson and Mill – had been arguing for votes for women all through the century; in its closing decades, the demand would become urgent, and suffragists – and later, militant suffragettes – would take centre stage.

Chapter 6

Fighting for the vote: suffragists

In the course of the 19th century, the vote gradually became central to feminist demands. It was seen as important both symbolically (as a recognition of women's rights to full citizenship) and practically (as a necessary way of furthering reforms and making practical changes in women's lives). But winning the vote proved a complicated struggle, and one that lasted for decades. The determination and the persistence with which women argued, and increasingly demonstrated, for the right to vote makes an inspiriting story; all the more so given the equal determination, and at times the virulence, with which their claims were opposed. And opposed, often, by women as well as men.

There had been some early demands for women's suffrage: William Thompson, influenced by Anna Wheeler, had eloquently made the case for their representation as early as 1825. Marion Reid, writing in 1843, dismissed current clichés about woman's proper 'sphere', as well as the notion that woman's supposed influence over man gave her everything she needed. She went on to stress the importance, not just of the vote, but of even a token presence in parliament. Perhaps 'a few women among the constituents of members of parliament' might induce that body 'to pay some little attention on the interests of women'. In 1847, an elderly Quaker, Anne Knight, issued a pamphlet arguing for women's right to be represented. Harriet Taylor, who became John Stuart Mill's wife, argued for 'The

Enfranchisement of Women' in the *Westminster Review* in 1851; while in 1869, Mill himself made the case eloquently and at some length in *The Subjection of Women*. Women, he conceded, are not likely to differ from men of the same class; but 'if the question be one in which the interests of women as such are in some way involved', then they 'require the suffrage, as their guarantee of just and equal consideration'.

There was, of course, nothing like complete male suffrage at this period. Even as late as the 1870s, only about one-third of adult men could vote, and though the Reform Act of 1884 increased that number, still only somewhere between 63% and 68% of men were enfranchised. But, ironically, the legal position of women had actually worsened with the Reform Act of 1832, which specifically excluded women by substituting 'male person' for the more inclusive and general word 'man', which, it could be argued, might be interpreted as meaning 'human being'. In the same year, a radical known as 'Orator' Hunt was asked to present parliament with a petition (which had been drawn up by a wealthy Yorkshire spinster called Mary Smith) arguing that 'every unmarried female possessing the necessary pecuniary qualifications' should be allowed to vote. The petitioner, Hunt pointed out, paid taxes like any man; moreover, since women could be *punished* at law, they should be given a voice in the *making* of laws, as well as the right to serve on juries.

But the struggle for the vote was only beginning, and it was never straightforward. There were divisions between those arguing for adult suffrage, and those who wanted to campaign simply on behalf of women. And amongst the latter, there was disagreement about *which* women should be enfranchised. Many early demands for women's suffrage concentrated on spinsters; Frances Power Cobbe, for example, argued the case for women property owners and taxpayers. These limited demands were partly a matter of tactics (if *some* women won the vote, it would at least set a precedent, which might later be more easily extended), but it was often assumed, dismissively, that a wife's interests were identical with her husband's, and that giving her a vote would simply mean handing a second one to the man of the household. Some women believed that the passing of a married women's property act would prove more immediately useful to them than the vote. On the other hand, Mrs Humphrey Ward expressed her anxiety that, if spinsters were allowed to vote, it would mean that 'large numbers of women leading immoral lives will be enfranchised, while married women, who, as a rule have passed through more of the practical experiences of life than the unmarried would be excluded'. One member of parliament remarked sarcastically that if spinsters were enfranchised, it would be rewarding 'that portion of the other sex which for some cause had failed to be womanly'. Other opponents of female suffrage argued that only a man might be called upon to fight for his country, and that 'gives him a claim of some sort to have a voice in the conduct of its affairs'.

The debate offers some odd and revealing glimpses into attitudes towards women. Thus in 1871, the political philosopher Thomas Carlyle remarked that

> the true destiny of a woman . . . is to wed a man she can love and esteem and to lead noiselessly, under his protection, with all the wisdom, grace and heroism that is in her, the life presented in consequence.

And a great many women, as well, accepted the notion that by nature and God's decree, women were different to men. God meant them to be wives and mothers; if they deserted their proper sphere, it would lead to 'a puny, enfeebled and sickly race'.

Progress, perhaps inevitably, proved very slow. Indeed, very many prominent women dismissed the vote as relatively unimportant, insisting, sometimes a shade disingenuously, that they, personally, had never suffered any disabilities from its lack. Florence Nightingale announced in 1867 that 'in the years that I have passed in Government offices, I have never felt the want of a vote', and though she later conceded its importance, she always felt there were other more urgent problems facing women. The successful writer and journalist Harriet Martineau insisted that 'the best friends of the cause are the happy wives and the busy, cheerful satisfied single women . . . whatever a woman proves herself able to do, society will be thankful to see her do'.

Beatrix Potter attributed her own 'anti-feminism' to 'the fact that I had never myself suffered the disabilities assumed to arise from my sex'. The Liberal Violet Markham came up with an evasive paradox: many women are clearly 'superior to men, and therefore I don't like to see them trying to become man's equals'. By 1889, the popular novelist and journalist Mrs Humphrey Ward was claiming that 'the emancipating process has now reached the limits fixed by the physical constitution of women'. Queen Victoria was sometimes hailed by suffragists as an example of what a woman was capable of; Barbara Leigh Smith, for example, pointed out that 'our gracious Queen fulfils the very arduous duties of her calling and manages also to be the mother of many children'. But Victoria notoriously exclaimed in horror against the 'mad wicked folly of women's rights'.

The Langham Place circle around Barbara Leigh Smith played an important part in the long struggle for the vote, as in so many other campaigns. Early in 1866, they organized a suffrage petition, with 1,499 signatures, which argued that 'person' should be substituted for 'man', and that all householders, without distinction of sex, should be enfranchised. Emily Davies, who had worked so effectively for women's education, formally handed the petition to John Stuart Mill, whose book *The Subjection of Women* had just been published, and he presented it to parliament in June 1866. It was – as they had expected – defeated, by 194 votes to 73; but even this was welcomed as an encouraging start. Its effectiveness was perhaps confirmed by the number of hostile responses it attracted. *The Spectator*, for example, sneered that no more than twenty women in the country were politically capable; women in general made political discussion 'unreal, tawdry, dressy'.

In October 1866, Leigh Smith and a group of friends met at Elizabeth Garrett's home in London to form a suffrage committee, which, the following year, became the London Society for Women's Suffrage. They organized petitions which brought together more than 3,000 signatures. Leigh Smith also produced a pamphlet on 'Reasons for the Enfranchisement of Women'; several establishment papers, including the *Cornhill* and the *Fortnightly Review*, refused to print the argument for women's votes. Around the same time, a woman called Lydia Becker formed a similar society in Manchester; she had been drawn to the cause after hearing a paper given by Leigh Smith; she formed a local Women's Suffrage Committee, and in 1870 founded the *Women's Suffrage Journal*. Pro-suffrage groups soon followed in Edinburgh, Bristol, and Birmingham; they proved important in keeping the issue alive through the decades ahead, and keeping up pressure on parliament. Public meetings were arranged, particularly in London and Manchester. Richard Pankhurst, who was involved in the Manchester group, had founded the *Englishwoman's Review* in 1866, and this helped publicize the suffragists' cause.

It was perhaps inevitable that the suffragists were at times plagued by disagreements, particularly about tactics; Barbara Leigh Smith soon withdrew from any formal participation in the London committee – she disagreed with John Stuart Mill and Harriet Taylor, who insisted that it was useful to have men on the committee – though she later served as its nominal secretary. For all his early support, Mill shrank back nervously from later developments and more aggressive tactics; he disapproved, particularly, of the 'common vulgar motives and tactics' of some women in Manchester. And the campaign to win the vote was to prove more difficult, and much longer-drawn-out, than its early supporters could have predicted. The issue was debated in parliament (and defeated) year after year, all through the 1870s. One Tory remarked in 1871 that women – who were sensitive and emotional by nature – should be protected 'from being forced into the hurly-burly of party politics'. Woman's proper sphere was the home; her duty – and her deepest pleasure – to be a good wife, or sister, or daughter. Moreover, if women had much influence in parliament, it would lead to 'hasty alliances with scheming neighbours, more class cries, permissive legislation, domestic perplexities and sentimental grievances'. The largest vote in favour of women's enfranchisement came in 1873, with 157 men in agreement.

Suffrage abroad

At the same time, British suffragists (and their opponents) watched developments abroad with interest. One woman remarked that 'scarcely anything does more good to women's suffrage in England than seeing those who speak from personal experience'. In fact, Antipodean examples seemed particularly encouraging. In New Zealand, women could vote from 1893; in Australia, state after state granted women the vote during the 1890s, until in 1902 women could finally vote in Federal elections. A conservative (male) professor remarked, darkly, in 1904, that 'I think Australia is doomed'. (On the other hand, Australian Aboriginals, male or female, could not vote until the late 1960s.) In America, the states, one by one, enfranchised white women; by 1914, women could vote in 11 states, though they had to wait until 1919 for the national vote. Denmark enfranchised women in 1915, and the Netherlands in 1919.

It is hardly surprising, given contemporary beliefs about a woman's role, that, for decades, suffragists achieved only small and undramatic victories, though, in the long run, these would prove very important in winning over public opinion. But, in the face of rejection and ridicule, they persisted. At the same time, many women were gaining experience and confidence by taking increasingly active roles in local government and other public bodies; they served on school boards and poor-law boards. And they were learning to speak in public; as the suffragist Lady Amberley once remarked, 'people expressed surprise to me afterwards to see that a woman could lecture and still look like a lady'. Moreover, the campaigning women emerged from every political persuasion, with Conservatives like Frances Power Cobbe and Emily Davies as committed to the cause as Liberal and Radical women.

By the 1890s, as a growing number of men were enfranchised, women's sense of disparity and injustice increased sharply. They pointed out that men who were poor and barely literate had been given the vote, while well-educated women, who paid rates and taxes, were still excluded from full citizenship. It has been argued that 1897 saw a real breakthrough: a bill in the House of Commons received a majority of 71 in favour of women, and the pattern was repeated in following years. None of this was translated into actual reform, but suffragists certainly felt encouraged.

Chapter 7

Fighting for the vote: suffragettes

The term 'suffragette' was coined in 1906 by the *Daily Mail*; it was a derogatory label that the growing militant movement adopted as their own and transformed. It was only very gradually that some suffragists, at least, had come to realize that they were achieving very little by peaceful means. But as early as 1868, Lydia Becker had claimed, dramatically but with some insight, that 'it *needs* deeds of bloodshed or violence' before the government can be 'roused to do justice'.

By the early 1870s, a few women were taking the idea of 'no taxation without representation' literally, and refusing to pay. But there was little real change until 1903, when the Women's Social and Political Union (WSPU) was founded by the Pankhurst family. They had already been protesting actively in their native Manchester against attempts to ban meetings held by the Independent Labour Party. Dr Pankhurst had in 1870 drafted the first Women's Disabilities Removal Bill, which was then presented to parliament by Jacob Bright. (It passed on a second reading, but was quashed by William Gladstone.) Mrs Emmeline Pankhurst had served as a Poor Law Guardian, and had remarked that 'though I had been a suffragist before I now began to think about the vote in women's hands not only as a right, but as a desperate necessity'. Her daughter Christabel had probably been influenced, not only by her parents but by listening to, and writing a profile of, the American suffragist

5. The cover of Ethel Smyth's 1911 song-sheet for the WSPU proclaims 'The March of the Women' towards the vote. She uses the suffragette colours – green, purple, and white – but this is a celebration, as much as a demonstration, full of hope for a better future.

Susan B. Anthony, who visited Manchester in 1902. Christabel wrote that, 'it is unendurable to think of another generation of women wasting their lives for the vote. We must not lose any more time. We must act.'

The WSPU would remain, in essence, a family organization, though in 1906 it was Fred and Emmeline Pethick Lawrence who agreed to finance the cause, and found it headquarters in Clement's Inn in London. (The WSPU is certainly the best-known, and was perhaps the most effective, group fighting for the vote, but there were many others – the Women's Freedom League, the National Union of Women's Suffrage Societies, the Actresses' Franchise League – who may have been less high-profile, but did make progress.) From the start, Christabel Pankhurst dominated the WSPU, and soon a circle of devoted followers gathered around her. They included the former mill girl Annie Kenney, who was soon recognized as one of their most effective speakers; a married woman and working-class Scot, Flora Drummond; and a socialist teacher, Teresa Billington.

Less than a year later, the WSPU had something like 58 branches; it had also suffered the first of what would prove numerous splits and revolts against Christabel. She was undoubtedly charismatic, and inspired a sometimes unhealthy devotion among her many followers. But she was often dictatorial and ruthless, and so, perhaps to a lesser extent, was her mother Emmeline. Teresa Billington later remarked that Christabel exploited her followers; that 'she took advantage of both their strengths and their weaknesses and laid on them the burden of unprepared action, refused to excuse weakness, boomed and boosted the novice into sham maturity, refused maturity a hearing'.

One woman, looking back in 1935, described Emmeline Pankhurst as 'a forerunner of Lenin, Hitler and Mussolini – the leader whose fiat must go unquestioned, the leader who could do no wrong'. There may well be truth in her angry exaggeration; and the same thing could be said, probably more accurately, of Christabel. She was, Teresa Billington remarked, 'a most astute statesman, a skilled politician, a self-dedicated re-shaper of the world, and a dictator without mercy'. Certainly, two of the WSPU's most dedicated and effective organizers, Fred and Emmeline Pethick Lawrence, would be expelled from the organization in 1914, and even Sylvia Pankhurst was pushed out, in 1913. Sylvia was probably the most interesting, and certainly the most sympathetic, member of the family: a talented artist, and a socialist, who formed her own East London Federation (ELF) in an attempt to reach out to working-class women with families. She was the partner of the Labour politician Keir Hardie, who risked his own career by supporting votes for women.

The shift towards militant action was gradual. The suffragettes began by heckling politicians at public meetings; they moved on to organizing their own mass meetings and processions. From the start, they displayed a remarkable instinct for the propaganda effects of spectacle; they rapidly became adept at making their points visually and dramatically. There were mass marches through the streets and demonstrations outside the Albert Hall, in Hyde Park: these public gatherings of women were, in Edwardian London, startling enough by themselves.

The suffragette colours were deployed effectively: the women dressed in white with green and purple sashes, and carried vividly colourful embroidered or appliquéd banners. The Artists' Suffrage League created dramatically effective posters and postcards. One of the best known has two layers: on the top, with the label 'What a Woman may be and yet not have the vote', are the figures of a nurse, a mother, a doctor, and a factory hand; the lower layer, 'What a man may have been and yet not lose the vote', includes a convict, a lunatic, a white slaver, a drunkard, and (rather unfairly) a cripple described as 'unfit for service'. Some of their propaganda was too sensational to be really effective: for example, a poster against the Cat and Mouse Act (relating to the release then re-arrest of hunger strikers from prison), which featured a vicious ginger cat, its teeth

6. **Suffragette demonstration, led by the Pankhursts, 1911.**

around the limp body of a woman dressed in the WSPU colours. And some suffragettes, at least, seem to have been acutely aware of the possible political opportunities offered by that still comparatively new form, photography, and exploited it very effectively. Indeed, it is perhaps the photographic and visual record that they left behind them that makes the suffragettes still seem so immediately interesting. Old black and white photographs of marches and demonstrations make the period come to vivid life – and so do images that capture what was seen as police persecution. One famous photograph shows Mrs Pankhurst, looking small and fragile in her meticulously draped, formal clothes, being carried off by two angry and brutal-looking men.

It was only gradually that the suffragettes then turned to direct action. They began with what seem to have been mild physical confrontations: banging at politicians' doors, or turning up en masse to protest at Downing Street. Feeling increasingly frustrated, they turned to sporadic acts of violence and arson: suffragettes began to set fire to letterboxes and smashed shop windows. Emmeline Pankhurst once remarked that 'the argument of the broken pane of glass is the most valuable argument in modern politics'. (Intriguingly, some of the West End shops whose windows were broken still advertised in the suffragette paper; some offered clothes in WSPU colours, and one even sold underwear in white, purple and green.)

According to Sylvia Pankhurst, who apparently approved, 'three Scottish castles were destroyed by fire in on a single night'. In early 1914, the Carnegie Library was burnt down, as well as two ancient churches and many large empty houses. Mary Richardson slashed Velázquez's painting of the Rokeby Venus in the National Gallery, announcing that 'I have tried to destroy the picture of the most beautiful woman in mythological history because the Government are destroying Mrs. Pankhurst – the most beautiful character in modern history'. Some militants went even further; they set fire to the house of a minister who was hostile to the cause, and two

7. Emmeline Pankhurst was arrested outside Buckingham Palace in May 1914, after trying to present a petition to the King. The man on the left looks frighteningly angry; the uniformed policeman is perhaps just doing his job.

women actually tried to burn down a crowded theatre in Dublin. And one woman, Emily Wilding Davison, died for the vote. Having declared that 'a tragedy was wanted' for the cause, on Derby Day 1913, she rushed onto the course in the middle of the race – certainly risking, or even inviting, death – and brought down the King's horse. She died of her injuries a few days later. But although, initially, the militants, and even fanatics like Davison, had aroused real sympathy, they were also managing to alienate many supporters.

Not everyone, even within the movement, agreed with the new, and escalating, tactics, which meant that increasing numbers of women were going to prison. Teresa Billington, who had formerly worked closely with Emmeline Pankhurst, denounced the adoption of

8. Emily Davison sacrifices herself for the cause, and dies after throwing herself under the King's horse on Derby Day 1913.

violence, which would 'condemn a large number of women to personal sacrifice that in some cases amounts to suicide, and in all cases to the suffering of terrible strain and much possible abuse'. She argued that militancy was thereby 'degraded from revolution into political chicanery', and denounced the 'pose of martyrdom' and the way suffragettes were presenting themselves 'not as rebels but as innocent victims'. Elizabeth Garrett Anderson resigned from the WSPU, and even Adela Pankhurst argued against extreme militancy. Divisions within the movement therefore increased.

As early as 1908, suffragettes who had been imprisoned for some form of direct or violent action had begun protesting against the authorities by going on hunger strikes. The first few women were released, but as more joined in, the authorities began to force-feed them. Many saw themselves, and were seen by many others, as martyrs. Emmeline Pankhurst went to gaol several times, and so did the Pethick Lawrences. Lady Constance Lytton had first been gaoled in 1909, but realizing that her rank had ensured her better treatment, when she was released she disguised herself, was sentenced again, and force-fed eight times. Her health was permanently damaged. The passage of the Prisoners' Temporary Discharge Bill, popularly know as the Cat and Mouse Act, aroused great controversy: women were released from prison until they recovered their health, at which point they were re-arrested. They aroused wide and genuine sympathy, but, as time went on, there was increasing criticism of their campaign, even from former supporters. Teresa Billington, for example, decided: 'I do not believe that the best avenue for the emancipation of women is through emotionalism, personal tyranny and fanaticism.'

By this stage, Christabel Pankhurst had long retreated from the fight. She was in Paris, where she led a life of ease and even luxury, avoiding the increasing perplexities faced by suffragettes at home. 'Ladies!' she had proclaimed in 1910, 'The truce was all very well, but there is nothing like militancy. We glory in this fight because we feel how much it strengthens us.' The devoted Annie Kenney visited

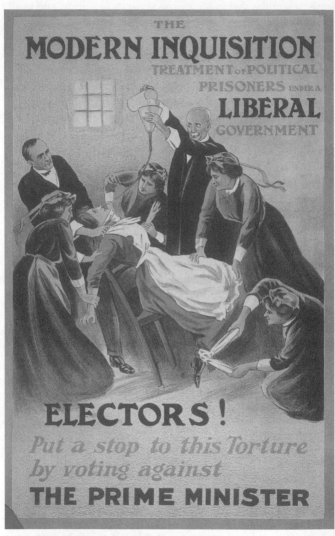

9. Poster dramatizing the condition of the suffragette prisoners being force-fed, 1910.

her every weekend, bringing back instructions from the leader in exile; other, more clear-sighted women were, very justly, critical of her absence.

The situation changed forever as a result of the First World War. In August 1914 Emmeline Pankhurst sensibly announced that the campaign for the vote was suspended. Christabel – whose sojourn in France seemed to have atrophied her ability to think clearly – remarked melodramatically that 'a man-made civilisation, hideous and cruel in time of peace, is to be destroyed'. The war, she continued, was 'God's vengeance upon the people who held women in subjection'. Sylvia, always far more thoughtful, remarked in *The Suffragette Movement* that

> men and woman had been drawn closer together by the suffering and sacrifice of the war. Awed and humbled by the great catastrophe, and by the huge economic problems it had thrown into naked prominence, the women of the suffrage movement had learnt that social regeneration is a long and mighty work.

In 1918, women over the age of 30 were given the vote; and in March 1928, under a Conservative government, they finally won it on equal terms with men.

Chapter 8
Early 20th-century feminism

During the early 20th century, English women achieved legal and civil equality, in theory if not always in practice. Some women, those over the age of 30, were allowed to vote from 1918, and there were arguments about whether their priority was to press hard for enfranchisement on the same terms as men, or to concentrate on women's other needs and problems. Some women, and some men, felt that a woman's party might have helped them build on the gains they had already achieved, but the opportunity was let slip.

The effects of the First World War had been so complex that it is impossible to generalize about them. It had allowed some women the opportunity to work outside the home; in the war years, the number of women employed outside the home rose by well over a million. Some worked in munitions factories and engineering works, others were employed in hospitals; many demanded pay rises, sometimes insisting their wages should be equal to men's. A Women's Volunteer Reserve was formed, and there were some Women's Police Patrols. Their contribution during the war, both domestically and as workers outside the home, almost certainly contributed to their partial enfranchisement in 1918. But many women were left widowed or unmarried, and the war-time press had talked darkly about 'flaunting flappers'. Sylvia Pankhurst commented, sarcastically, that 'alarmist morality-mongers conceived most monstrous visions of girls and women . . . plunging into excesses and burdening the country with swarms of illegitimate children'. One feminist paper remarked that military authorities did not realize that 'in protecting the troops from the women, they have failed to protect the women from the troops'.

As early as 1918, MPs agreed that women could actually sit in parliament, though it was only slowly that women were actually elected. Christabel Pankhurst stood for Smethwick in 1918, but lost by 700 votes. In 1919 and 1920, two women – the Conservative Lady Astor and the Liberal Margaret Wintringham – succeeded to their husbands' seats. Astor had never been particularly involved in the long struggle for the suffrage, but Wintringham had been a member of the National Union of Societies for Equal Citizenship (NUSEC), and also of the Women's Institute. She went on to proclaim, publicly, that homemaking was a 'privileged, skilled and nationally important occupation'.

The Labour Party member Ellen Wilkinson – an unmarried woman with a trade union background – was elected in 1924, and she was impressively outspoken on a whole range of issues; she was keenly interested in women's domestic role and argued for family allowances; she supported trade union rights; and she was a member of an International League for Peace and Freedom delegation that investigated reports of cruelty by British soldiers in Ireland. 'The men come in the middle of the night and the women are driven from their beds without any clothing other than a coat', she wrote: 'They are run out in the middle of the night and the home is burned.'

In 1929, Lady Astor suggested that women MPs form a women's party, but the notion fizzled out when Labour women were reluctant to support the idea. (Some modern historians have argued that this was a real opportunity that was thrown away.) As late as 1940, when a coalition government was formed, there were only 12 women MPs. Local government seemed a more favourable area for politically concerned women. Ever since the 1870s, women had been actively serving on school boards and other local bodies, and their numbers increased after the war.

NUSEC's broader aim had been to 'obtain all other reforms, economic, legislative and social as are necessary to secure a real equality of liberties, status and opportunities between men and women'. Its members campaigned, for example, to open the professions to women, and argued their right to equal pay. In 1919, the Sex Discrimination (Removal) Act, in theory at least, opened the professions and the civil service to women. According to Virginia Woolf, the Act did more for women than the franchise, but modern historians have expressed doubts, at least about its short-term efficacy. In 1923, a Matrimonial Causes Act established equal grounds for divorce between men and women.

But NUSEC was concerned, not simply with equality, but with *difference*; its members tried to tackle women's special problems and needs. When Eleanor Rathbone became president, she argued that women should demand, not equality with men, but 'what women need to fulfil the potentialities of their own natures and to adjust themselves to the circumstances of their own lives'. Their demands included reform of the laws governing divorce, the guardianship of children, and prostitution. In 1921, the Six Point Group was founded; it included some former militants, including the journalist and novelist Rebecca West, but its demands, and methods, were hardly radical. They too addressed women's special problems, arguing for a better deal for unmarried women, and for widows with children, as well as reform of the law on child assault. They wanted equal rights of guardianship for married men and women, equal pay for women teachers, and they challenged discrimination against women in the civil service. They issued a blacklist of MPs hostile to women's interests, urging women, whatever their political loyalties, to vote against them.

Several new magazines directed at women appeared in the 1920s, though their titles – *Woman and Home, Good Housekeeping* –

clearly signal the limited expectations of their audience. But there were also dissenting voices, with a more radical take on women's position, in *Time and Tide*, which was launched in 1920, its distinguished contributors including Virginia Woolf, Rebecca West, and Rose Macaulay. This magazine argued that women should act, independently, to put pressure on *all* the political parties to tackle women's concerns, and it raised a whole range of women's issues, including the position of unmarried mothers and of widows, and the guardianship of children. West wrote in 1925, as so often deliberately provocative:

> I am an old fashioned feminist, . . . when those of our army whose voices are inclined to coolly tell us that the day of sex-antagonism is over and henceforth we have only to advance hand in hand with the male, I do not believe it.

West was a socialist and a suffragist, an effective propagandist who always enjoyed a scrap – and who believed that women still had plenty to fight about.

But her writing covers a whole range of subjects, and she is perceptive and often sharply witty. She mocks masculine sentimentality about women: 'If we want to make every woman a Madonna we must see that every woman has quite a lot to eat', she remarked, but she is equally scathing about idle upper-class women who spend days 'loafing about the house with only a flabby mind for company'.

In later years Rebecca West went on to write very effectively on the trials of Nazi war criminals; and in the late 1930s produced a long and very interesting book on Yugoslavia. Her novels, on the other hand, reveal an unexpected and often cloying sentimentality about the relations between men and women. Perhaps this sprang from what seems to have been an unhappy private life: she had an illegitimate child by H. G. Wells and, though they stayed together for a few years, she essentially brought up her son Anthony alone. He later turned nastily on his mother, apparently without any understanding of what must have been a difficult time for her.

All through this period, the popular press, whether nervously or sarcastically, tended to portray the feminist as a frustrated spinster or a harridan; one journalist remarked that, because of war, many young women 'have become so de-sexed and masculinised, indeed, and the neuter states so patent in them, that the individual is described (unkindly) no longer as "she" but "it"'. Women teachers, as well as women in the civil service, sometimes had to fight against discrimination. The 1920s also saw the beginnings of economic recession and, as so often, women were the first to face unemployment.

But there were certainly more women being adequately educated, at schools and also at university level, thanks in large part to the work of Emily Davies (see Chapter 5). However, in *A Room of One's Own*, Virginia Woolf, in her typically oblique way, suggested the ways in which women were second-class citizens in Cambridge: she describes being barred from entering a famous library, and how she and a friend, a fellow in a women's college, dined, not like the men on sole and partridge, but on gravy soup and beef. In 1935 another writer, Dorothy L. Sayers, gave in her novel *Gaudy Night* a much more generous and affectionate account – based on her own education at Somerville College, Oxford – of the integrity, high intelligence, and conscientious concern for other people shown by the women dons (even though she had to import her male detective to sort out a criminal problem for them). As one of her dons remarks, cheerfully, they have indeed achieved a great deal – and it has all been done by 'pennypinching'.

The battle for legal, civil, and educational equality has been – and to some extent still is – a central element in feminism; but the movement has also highlighted the differences between the sexes, and asked for a new and deeper understanding of women's special needs as wives and mothers. One of the most interesting – and in the long run, most significant – episodes in the early 20th century concerned a subject that had rarely been publicly discussed, and which could still arouse bitter opposition: contraception. As early as 1877, the pro-birth control organization the Malthusian League had issued propaganda about ways of controlling conception; two of its most prominent members, Annie Besant and Charles Bradlaugh, were put on trial for publishing an American tract on the subject, called *The Law of Population*. (This was the same Annie Besant who became a vociferous supporter of the strike of female workers over conditions at the Bryant and May match factories in the 1880s.)

The Law of Population was written by Margaret Sanger, who had worked as a nurse with women in the New York slums, as well as setting up a monthly magazine, *Woman Rebel*, which not only called for revolution but – apparently more dangerously – also offered contraceptive information. In a pamphlet called *Family Limitation*, she argued that contraception enabled 'the average woman' to have 'a mutual and satisfied sexual act . . . the magnetism of it is health-giving and acts as a beautifier and tonic'. Sanger left the United States the day before she was due to be tried under the Comstock Law, which, in 1873, had made it an offence to send 'obscene, lewd or lascivious' material through the mail. She arrived in Glasgow in 1914, then came to London in July 1915, where she met Marie Stopes.

In spite of their shared interests, their relationship was by no means easy. Stopes was a complicated and difficult woman. As a girl, she had been both clever and ambitious, and, encouraged by her father, was educated to university level, gaining a BSc. But – presumably like many other well-brought-up girls of the period – she knew almost nothing about sexuality. Nevertheless, her very prolonged ignorance does seem unusual; after a long, intense, but sexless love affair with a Japanese man called Fujii, she married a man called Reginald Gates. This marriage was never consummated, but it took

10. Margaret Sanger, a nurse working with women in the New York slums, made contraceptive advice widely available – a very courageous act at the time – and had to flee the country to avoid court action against her.

her something like three years to realize that something was missing. Her second marriage, to Humphrey Roe, never proved quite as rapturous as she had hoped, though he gave her valuable support when she later opened a birth control clinic. But Stopes at least found effective ways of moving through her own ignorance to help other women who might be almost as uninformed as her younger self. She went on to write *Married Love* (1916), which sold 2,000 copies in a fortnight, and by the end of the year had reached six editions. It was followed by *Wise Parenthood* (1918) and *Radiant Motherhood* (1920). Her style was – well, flowery:

> the half swooning sense of flux which overtakes the spirit in that eternal moment at the apex of rapture sweeps into its flaming tides the whole essence of the man and woman.

This (not altogether convincing) bliss was in stark contrast to another, darker but equally fantastic, vision of

> the thriftless who breed so rapidly [and] tend by that very fact to bring forth children who are weakened and handicapped by physical as well as mental warping and weakness, and at the same time to demand their support from the sound and thrifty.

But Marie Stopes proved herself a loyal friend to Margaret Sanger. When Sanger returned to America and again faced prosecution, Stopes came to her support, not only organizing a petition on her behalf, but writing, with characteristic drama, to the President of the United States:

> Have you, Sir, visualized what it means to be a woman whose every fibre, whose every muscle and blood-capillary is subtly poisoned by the secret, ever growing horror, more penetrating, more long-drawn than any nightmare, of an unwanted embryo developing beneath her heart?

Marie Stopes's books – their practical side, at least, clearly answering an urgent need – continued to sell very well indeed. When she insisted that 'the normal man's sexual needs' are not 'stronger than the normal woman's', she obviously touched a chord in many other women. She and Reginald Gates went on to set up a birth control clinic in Holloway, North London, where poor women were offered free contraceptive advice. The clinic's brochure claimed that they were offering health and hygiene to the internally damaged 'slave mothers' who yearly produced their 'puny infants', but were 'callously left in coercive ignorance by the middle classes and the medical profession'. But Marie Stopes also managed to antagonize many of the people who shared her interests and who might have worked effectively with her. In 1928, one possible colleague complained that she was suffering from 'paranoia and megalomania'.

In 1936 a group of women tackled an even more controversial issue, when they founded the Abortion Law Reform Association. Something like 500 women a year were dying from abortions, they argued; and that was quite unnecessary. One of their campaigners, the Canadian-born Stella Browne, had the courage to admit publicly that 'if abortion was necessarily fatal or injurious, I should not be here before you'. The issue remained controversial into (and beyond) the 1950s, when several women's organizations began to press for the legalization of abortion. In 1956, a newspaper survey found that, out of 200 people questioned, 51.9% favoured abortion on request, and 23.4% for health reasons. But abortion remained a major, and often problematic, issue long after the revival of feminism in the 1970s.

Virginia Woolf has been dismissed as irrelevant by some contemporary feminists; Sheila Rowbotham, for example, remarks that her demand, in *A Room of One's Own*, for £500 a year and space to oneself was simply aimed at a minority of the educated middle class. That is true; but she is read still, and by women (and men) who would never so much as glance at most feminist writing. Woolf was certainly ambivalent about the term 'feminism'; she admitted that she was anxious, when the book was first published, that she might be 'attacked for a feminist'. In *Three Guineas* – a later and much darker book, written in the shadow of approaching war and the growth of fascism – Woolf directly attacks the word 'feminism'; it is 'an old word, a vicious and corrupt word that has done much harm in its day and is now obsolete'. Her plea to 'the daughters of educated men' – rather than simply to educated women – now sounds rather clumsy, and in the 1930s must have already been rather dated. (By educated men, she explains that she means those who had been at Oxford or Cambridge.) But she refers effectively and scathingly to 'Arthur's Education Fund' that for decades, even centuries, has allowed boys, but not their sisters, to be adequately taught; and she remarks sardonically that, until 1919, marriage has been 'the one great profession open to women'. Moreover, she adds, they were actually unfitted even for that by their lack of education.

In *A Room of One's Own*, Virginia Woolf defends Rebecca West, who had just been attacked by a man who labelled her an 'arrant feminist! She says that men are snobs!' The suffrage campaign, Woolf fears, 'must have roused in men an extraordinary desire for self-assertion'. After all, she remarks, 'women have served all these centuries as looking-glasses possessing the magic and delicious power of reflecting the figure of man at twice its natural size'. In fact, she insists, most women have little idea how much men actually hate them. 'The history of men's opposition to women's emancipation', she remarks dryly, 'is more interesting perhaps than the story of that emancipation itself. An amusing book might be made of it.' But the writer, she adds, 'would need thick gloves on her hands, and bars to protect her of solid gold'. And, after all, what seems amusing now 'had to be taken in desperate earnest once . . . Among your grandmothers and great-grandmothers there were many that wept their eyes out.'

Glancing at a modern novel by the fictional writer 'Mary Carmichael', Woolf comes upon the words 'Chloe liked Olivia', 'And then it struck me how immense a change was there. Chloe liked Olivia perhaps for the first time in literature.' That is to say, women in fiction up until that time had almost always been seen in relation to men. Reading on, Woolf learns that these two women share a laboratory, 'which of itself will make their friendship more varied and lasting because it will be less personal'. And she exclaims that Mary Carmichael may be lighting a torch where nobody has yet been, exploring a place where 'women are alone, unlit by the capricious and coloured light of the other sex'.

In perhaps the most memorable pages of *A Room of One's Own*, Virginia Woolf sums up her argument about how women's talents have been – and often still are – frustrated and wasted. She contemplates a number of greatly talented women from the past, from the Duchess of Newcastle to George Eliot and Charlotte Brontë – who were deprived of 'experience and intercourse and travel' and so never wrote quite as powerfully and generously as they might have done. Woolf invents the hauntingly effective figure of Shakespeare's sister, as gifted as her brother, but inevitably disappointed, mocked, and exploited by men. Like her brother, Judith arrived hopefully at the London theatres, but soon 'found herself with child . . . and so – who shall measure the heat and violence of the poet's heart when caught and tangled in a woman's body? – killed herself one winter's night and lies buried at some cross-roads where the omnibuses now stop outside the Elephant and Castle.' But 'she lives in you and in me, and in many other women who are not here tonight, for they are washing up the dishes and putting the children to bed'.

Chapter 9
Second-wave feminism: the late 20th century

What is sometimes termed 'second-wave' feminism emerged, after the Second World War, in several countries. In 1947, a Commission on the Status of Women was established by the United Nations, and two years later it issued a Declaration of Human Rights, which both acknowledged that men and women had 'equal rights as to marriage, during marriage and at its dissolution', as well as women's entitlement to 'special care and assistance' in their role as mothers. Between 1975 and 1985, the UN called three international conferences on women's issues, in Mexico City, Copenhagen, and Nairobi, where it was acknowledged that feminism

> constitutes the political expression of the concerns and interests of women from different regions, classes, nationalities, and ethnic backgrounds ... There is and must be a diversity of feminisms, responsive to the different needs and concerns of different women, and defined by them for themselves.

African women offered a salutary reminder that

> women are also members of classes and countries that dominate others ... Contrary to the best intentions of 'sisterhood', not all women share identical interests.

A remarkable variety of Western women picked up their pens. One of the most influential was, and remains, the French writer Simone de Beauvoir. Her writings – including four volumes of autobiography and several novels – add up to a remarkable exploration of one woman's experience; women from many other countries responded, saying that Beauvoir's *The Second Sex* (1949) had helped them to see their personal frustrations in terms of the general condition of women. All through history, Beauvoir argues, woman has been denied full humanity, denied the human right to create, to invent, to go beyond mere living to find a meaning for life in projects of ever-widening scope. Man 'remodels the face of the earth, he creates new instruments, he invents, he shapes the future'; woman, on the other hand, is always and archetypally Other. She is seen by and for men, always the object and never the subject.

Through chapters that range over the girl child, the wife, the mother, the prostitute, the narcissist, the lesbian, and the woman in love, Beauvoir explores different aspects of her central argument: it is *male* activity that in creating values has made of existence itself a value; this activity has prevailed over the confused forces of life; 'it has subdued Nature and Woman'. Woman, she argues, has come to stand for Nature, Mystery, the non-human; what she *represents* is more important than what she *is*, what she herself experiences.

But 'one is not born, but rather becomes, a woman', Beauvoir insists; and she can change her condition. Most women, mistakenly, look for salvation in love. But Beauvoir's own alternative is perhaps too simple: she conjures up an image of the 'the independent woman' who

> . . . wants to be active, a taker, and refuses the passivity man means to impose on her. The modern woman accepts masculine values; she prides herself on thinking, taking action, working, creating on the same terms as man.

That is not really an attractive image of our possible future. But, she adds rightly, too many women cling to the privileges of femininity; while too many men are comfortable with the limitations it imposes on women. Today, women are torn between the past and a possible, but difficult and as yet unexplored, future.

Beauvoir was always opposed to any feminism that championed women's special virtues or values, firmly rejecting any idealization of specifically 'feminine' traits. To support that kind of feminism, she argued, would imply agreement with

> a myth invented by men to confine women to their oppressed state. For women it is not a question of asserting themselves as women, but of becoming full-scale human beings.

But though Beauvoir was and remained critical of some forms of traditional feminism, she was impressed by the emerging Mouvement de Libération des Femmes (MLF), admitting in a 1972 interview that she recognized that

> it is necessary, before the socialism we dream of arrives, to struggle for the actual position of women . . . Even in socialist countries, this equality has not been obtained. Women must therefore take their destiny into their own hands.

Beauvoir was one of the women who signed a 1971 manifesto published in the *Nouvel Observateur*, drawn up by an MLF group, who were campaigning to legalize abortion; 343 women signed it, proclaiming 'I have had an abortion and I demand this right for all women.' However, she always insisted (not wholly convincingly) that she herself had no personal experience of women's 'wrongs', that she had escaped the oppression that she analyses so brilliantly in *The Second Sex*.

> Far from suffering from my femininity, I have, on the contrary, from the age of twenty on, accumulated the advantages of both sexes . . . those around me treated me both as a writer, their peer in the

masculine world, and as a woman . . . I was encouraged to write *The Second Sex* precisely because of this privileged position. It allowed me to express myself in all serenity.

11. Perhaps the most influential of all 20th-century Western feminists, Simone de Beauvoir remains important still, for her autobiographies and novels as well as for her great piece of feminist theory, *The Second Sex*.

But Beauvoir's four autobiographical volumes – *Memoirs of a Dutiful Daughter*, *The Prime of Life*, *The Force of Circumstance*, and *All Said and Done* – as well as the 1964 book about her mother, ironically entitled *A Very Easy Death*, take us on a uniquely detailed, remarkably frank, and often very moving journey through her own experiences. She never suggests that she is a model for others; but she evokes her own life as a successful example of how one girl escaped the feminine role of 'object, Other'. She is almost apologetic about concentrating on women's issues when 'some of us have never had to sense in our femininity an inconvenience or an obstacle'. But she admitted that a woman who takes up the pen inevitably provides

> a stick to be beaten with . . . if you are a young woman they indulge you with an amused wink. If you are old, they bow to you respectfully. But lose that bloom of youth and dare to speak before acquiring the respectable patina of age: the whole pack is at your heels.

And her autobiographies, as well as her novels, are all the more moving, and certainly speak more directly to women readers, because, perhaps against Beauvoir's conscious intentions, they evoke her own – inevitable – frustrations and uncertainties, whether about Jean-Paul Sartre's infidelities during their long relationship, about her own affairs with the American writer Nelson Algren and with Claude Lanzmann, or about her own childlessness.

But to the end, Beauvoir remained open to new experiences. In 1955, after she and Sartre visited China, she wrote *The Long March*, acknowledging that it had 'upset my whole idea of our planet', as she came to understand 'that our Western comfort [is] merely a limited privilege'. Her last major theoretical work, *Old Age* (1970), in which she struggles to maintain her cool rationality in the face of the ultimate, the inevitable, defeat, is perhaps her most moving book.

Betty Friedan's 1963 book *The Feminine Mystique* exploded the myth of the happy housewife in the affluent, white, American suburbs; 'the problem that has no name', she wrote, 'burst like a boil through the image of the happy American Mystique'. The idea for the book began with a magazine article she wrote after she had attended a class reunion, and asked other women there, 'what do you wish you had done differently?' Their answers alerted her to a vague but pervasive discontent. She has been criticized, correctly, for being narrowly middle class; for a simplistic argument that urges suburban women to plan their lives ahead so that they can move from family duties to work outside the home, while ignoring the numbers of less fortunate women already desperately juggling housework with outside jobs, usually poorly paid. For poorer Americans, the black feminist bell hooks argued:

> liberation means the freedom of a mother finally to quit her job – to live the life of a capitalist stay at home, as it were . . . To be able to work and to have to work are two very different matters.

But Friedan's book was a well-researched, sharply written, even passionate indictment of the fact that *even* affluent middle-class women lead restricted lives, and too often lapse into a depressed acceptance of that restriction. She insisted that each woman must at least *ask* what she truly wants. Then she may indeed realize that 'neither her husband nor her children nor the things in her house, nor sex, nor being like all the other women, can give her a self'.

Friedan's own background had been in radical politics, and her earlier writings, particularly, display a keen awareness of social inequalities. Moreover, with a group of other women, some from the Union of the Automobile Workers, she went on to become one of the founder members of NOW, the National Organization of Women, which set out 'to bring women into full participation in the mainstream of American society, now, assuming all the privileges and responsibilities thereof in truly equal partnership with men'.

12. Betty Friedan in New York, 1970.

Friedan, like some of the older women in the movement, was concerned that the new feminist rhetoric 'rigidified in reaction against the past, harping on the same old problems in the same old way', instead of moving forward. In *The Second Stage* (1981) she admits both how much has changed for women – and how little. Despite arduous and prolonged attempts to get the Equal Rights Amendment passed, some states still reject it. Perhaps inevitably, there was a widening gap between Friedan and the new generation of feminists, though it is hardly fair to accuse her of going along with a 'backlash'. She approvingly quotes a Toronto journalist:

> I don't want to be stuck today with a feminist label anymore than I would want to be known as a 'dumb blonde' in the fifties. The libber label limits and short-changes those who are tagged with it. And the irony is that it emerged from a philosophy that set out to destroy the notion of female tagging.

Her criticism may be unfair, but it cannot be dismissed out of hand.

Within Western feminism – or Women's Liberation as it soon came to be called – there was initially, at least, great variety, and an energy that sprang in part from anger at having been excluded in existing leftist groups, in part from fruitful disagreements within the emerging movement itself. Many younger women – in the student movement, amongst anti-Vietnam protesters and New Left activists – had felt they were being sidelined by their male comrades. Women among the American Students for a Democratic Society (SDS) announced in 1965 that, having learned 'to think radically about the personal worth and abilities of people whose role in society had gone unchallenged before', a lot of women in the movement 'have begun trying to apply those lessons to their relations with men'. Two years later, SDS women insisted that their 'brothers . . . recognize that they must deal with their own problems of male chauvinism'. Some women issued a news-sheet called 'Voice of the Women's Liberation Movement', along with a manifesto from New Left activists who found themselves sidelined by male comrades, and who were infuriated by Stokely Carmichael's infamous remark that 'the place of women in the movement is prone'.

bell hooks, in her *Feminist Theory: From Margin to Centre* (1984), was sharply critical of the whole movement, arguing that the women 'who are most victimized by sexist oppression . . . who are powerless to change their condition in life' have never been allowed to speak out for themselves. Current feminism, she insists, is racist, and has left many women bitterly disillusioned. Movement women have consistently ignored the deeply intertwined issues of race and class; the emphasis on the common 'oppression' of women has in fact ignored terribly real inequalities within American society. White women behaved as if the movement belonged to them, hooks insists; they ignored the fact that women are divided by all kinds of prejudice, 'by sexist attitudes, racism, class privilege'. hooks recalls her own experience in feminist groups: 'I found that white women adopted a condescending attitude towards me and other non white participants.' Black feminists rightly argue that 'every problem raised by white feminists has a disproportionately heavy impact on blacks'.

In America, expressions of feminism ranged from Gloria Steinem's accessible and glossy *Ms* magazine, first published in 1970, to the Sisterhood of Black Single Mothers. In her book *Sexual Politics* (1970), Kate Millett set out to analyse 'patriarchy as a *political* institution'. Politics, she insists, refers to all 'power structured relationships', and the one between the sexes is a 'relationship of dominance and subordinance' which has been largely unexamined. Women are simultaneously idolized and patronized, she argued, backing up her thesis with a scathing analysis of the patriarchal attitudes of writers from different periods and cultures: Freud, D. H. Lawrence, Henry Miller, Norman Mailer, and Jean Genet. She saw little immediate hope for women; 'it may be that we shall . . . be able to retire sex from the harsh realities of politics', she concluded, 'but not until we

have created a world we can bear out of the desert we inhabit'.
Other political statements included the American Shulamith
Firestone's *The Dialectic of Sex* (1970), which argued that the
basic division, the most profound oppression, in society was not
class but sex; she hoped for a true 'feminist revolution', but
argued that revolution would demand

> an analysis of the dynamics of sex war as comprehensive as the
> Marx-Engels analysis of class antagonism was for the economic
> revolution. More comprehensive, for we are dealing with a larger
> problem, with an oppression that goes back beyond recorded history
> to the animal kingdom itself.

In England, the Australian-born Germaine Greer's lively and
provocative *The Female Eunuch* (1970) challenged the 'sense of
inferiority or natural dependence' which women have too often
accepted placidly, passively, allowing it to distort and impoverish
their lives. There are chapters on the middle-class myth of love and
marriage; on why being 'an object of male fantasy' actually
desexualizes women, and on the way 'cooking, clothes, beauty and
housekeeping' can become compulsive, anxiety-producing
activities.

Sheila Rowbotham's *Liberation and the New Politics* (1970)
and Juliet Mitchell's *Woman's Estate* (1971) were both written in
response to the emerging Women's Liberation movement in
England. Though that movement, Mitchell argued, was
international 'in its identification and shared goals', and was
for the most part 'professedly, if variously, revolutionary'. Her
book cites, briefly, women's movements in Europe (Holland,
Sweden, and France) and in the United States. Everywhere, she
argues, women are 'the most fundamentally oppressed people and
hence potentially the most revolutionary', and she goes on to
examine four areas of their lives that must be transformed:
production, reproduction, sexuality, and the socialization of
children.

Lesbian feminism

In the late 1960s, many lesbians felt themselves sidelined both in the women's movement and in the emerging gay liberation groups. Betty Friedan, president of NOW, notoriously described women advocating lesbian issues as a 'lavender menace'. Her denigration was angrily rejected in a brief manifesto called *The Woman-Identified Woman*. In 1973, the well-known American journalist Jill Johnston published *Lesbian Nation: The Feminist Solution*, which included a witty satire on heterosexual romance: 'it begins when you sink into his arms, and ends with your arms in his sink'.

Some lesbians insisted that they were central to women's liberation because their very existence threatens male supremacy at its most vulnerable point. Lesbianism was sometimes suggested as the most, or even the only, politically correct choice for a woman. Rita Mae Brown argued that the difference between heterosexual and lesbian women was 'the difference between reform and revolution'. In *No Turning Back: Lesbian and Gay Liberation of the '80s*, the male and female writers attacked both the common assumption that every household should be heterosexual, as well as the widespread 'belief in the inherent inferiority of the dominant-male/passive-female role pattern'.

These writings sprang from, and encouraged, the new but rapidly growing women's movement, in various European countries including England, but also, and perhaps crucially, in America. Women within the Civil Rights Movement, the Black Movement, and Students for a Democratic Society complained that, too often, they were treated as 'typists, tea-makers and sexual objects'.

Protests at the Miss America contest in Atlantic City in November 1968 and in 1969, when feminists mockingly crowned a sheep, gave the emerging movement high visibility. Protesters argued that the beauty contest was a symbol of the way women in general are objectified, diminished, and judged primarily on appearance. 'Every day in a woman's life is a walking Miss World Contest', one feminist remarked wearily.

In London, women had been meeting in small groups since 1969: some had been involved in protesting against the war in Vietnam, and helping American deserters; other women emerged from traditional left-wing groups, from student movements, or from the radically experimental Anti-University. Hackney women began producing a news-sheet called *Shrew*, and later issues were put out by other London groups. By the end of 1971, *Shrew* listed 56 groups – plus one men's group. A conference had been called in February 1970 in Oxford; so many women and children (and a few men) turned up that the venue was shifted from Ruskin College to the Oxford Union. Above all, the meetings offered women the opportunity to talk: about loneliness, about equal rights at work, about childcare, about housework, about men, about revolution. The emerging movement, rather optimistically perhaps, defined its demands: equal pay, equal education and opportunity, 24-hour nurseries, and free contraception and abortion on demand. A big march through London was organized, with banners announcing 'we're not beautiful, we're not ugly, we're angry'.

It remained a mainly middle-class movement, though there were many attempts to communicate with working-class women: feminists offered their support to a night cleaners' campaign for better pay and conditions, and to a strike by women machinists at the Ford Dagenham plant.

Perhaps the most distinctive element in the new movement was its organization: women met in small groups, some locally based, others – later – formed to discuss particular issues, or work for

13. **All women are beautiful: demonstration against the Miss America pageant, Atlantic City, 1969.**

Body issues

One of the most urgent concerns of second-wave feminism has been a woman's rights over her own body. Western feminists have often addressed questions about beauty and the value placed on a woman's external appearance – an issue which may seem, but only at first glance, superficial. Partly driven by the tantalizingly glamorous media images that swamp us, some seek refuge in an anxious, often ruinously expensive, pursuit of the latest fashion. Others may turn to more desperate and self-destructive measures: dieting to the point of anorexia (which may alternate with compulsive eating and bulimia), or anxiously seeking the self-mutilation that is cosmetic surgery.

Susie Orbach's *Fat is a Feminist Issue* (1981) and Naomi Wolf's *The Beauty Myth* (1990) both explore the physical self-hatred and the fear of ageing that, understandably, plague so many contemporary women. And even in the affluent West, women have had to fight hard for the right to better health care: for adequate gynaecological advice and care in childbirth; for the right to contraception and, if necessary, abortion; and for more attention to those cancers, of the breast and the womb, for example, that particularly affect women.

particular causes. But most involved some kind of 'consciousness-raising'. The term had been coined by an American, Kathie Sarachild: women would meet regularly and talk from their own experience. It was to have nothing to do with gossip; groups set out to explore both what women had in common and the issues that

14. Women's Liberation groups marching through London, 1971.

divided them. The overall aim was to begin to understand private fears and discontents in a wider context, to discover, through 'sharing, recognizing, naming' their political implications. As Juliet Mitchell remarked, 'women come into the movement from the unspecific frustration of their own private lives, find what they thought was an individual dilemma is a social predicament'.

Consciousness-raising, Mitchell has suggested, was a matter of 'speaking the unspoken: the opposite, in fact, of "nattering together"'. Women who cannot deal with the peculiar forms oppression takes in their private lives are 'highly suspect when they begin to talk about forms of oppression that afflict other women . . . If we cannot face our own problems we have no right to claim that we have answers to other people's problems.' Men were excluded, not, for the most part, out of hostility, but out of a recognition that women have the habit of deferring to men, 'intellectually and/or flirtatiously', at least in public.

Consciousness-raising was never intended – as its detractors sometimes claimed – merely as 'group therapy'. At meetings, women would speak in turn about their problems and frustrations; not simply as an outlet for individual grievances, but, hopefully, as a step towards understanding that these may not simply be a result of their personal situations. It was to be a way of discovering what they had in common *as women*, whatever their differences of class or race or personal experience. (They were mostly, if not wholly, younger women, so differences of age were rarely addressed.)

As one American feminist remarked, 'consciousness-raising is a way of forming a political analysis on information we can trust is true. That information is our experience.' Another American, Shulamith Firestone, argued that 'agitation for specific freedoms is worthless without the preliminary raising of consciousness necessary to utilize these freedoms in full'. Other women were less certain about it all. Some complained that consciousness-raising was particularly suited to the educated women of the middle and upper classes, and

15. As this banner suggests, the early movement, in America as in Britain, quickly learned to make its arguments dramatically and wittily.

that these women were able to gain ascendancy over groups through their articulacy, their proficiency in this central activity. In fact, at the time, most women had little experience of group dynamics. Because the play of feelings within a group can be so unpredictable, even explosive, one or other member of a group might easily feel she was being unfairly criticized, made a scapegoat, or even excluded. Some meetings proved unexpectedly, and unhelpfully, painful. Sisterhood may be powerful; it was sometimes forgotten that the relationship between sisters may prove a troubled one. There were, inevitably, splits and disagreements. In England, one early conference was split – improbable as may sound – by a bitter quarrel between lesbian feminists and Maoist feminists. At another weekend conference, held in a building that was shared by a large group of coal miners, some women, who obviously had little clue about working-class men or about how to deflect their teasing aggression, began shouting that 'sisters are being brutalized by the miners'.

But (real) male violence was a problem that urgently needed to be raised. Some feminists, particularly in America., disappointed by the failure to ensure passage of the Equal Rights Amendment and by threats to welfare and abortion rights, seized on this issue as a symbol of woman's second-class status and her vulnerability. In 1975, the American Susan Brownmiller published a long, scholarly, and ground-breaking study of rape, *Against Our Will*, which deconstructed the centuries-old male 'myth of the heroic rapist', and coined a slogan that was rapidly picked up by other feminists: 'pornography is the theory and rape the practice'. (One of those feminists was Susan Griffin, who made an effective attack on the easy and commonplace way people justify pornography, by claiming that is it 'liberating' for women as well as for men. In *Pornography and Silence* (1981), she argued that, far from freeing erotic energy, as its defenders claimed, pornography expresses 'fear of bodily knowledge and a desire to silence eros'.) Brownmiller went on to argue that rape is nothing more or less than a conscious process of intimidation used against *all* women by *all* men. She is not sentimental about women; her later book, *Femininity*, deconstructs, disconcertingly and wittily, the games girls learn almost from the cradle: the tricks and techniques for charming men and competing with other women. Femininity, as we know it, is romantic nonsense, something that has to be carefully contrived and preserved. It is the product of 'a nostalgic tradition of imposed limitation'. But *Against Our Will* mocks, bitterly and effectively, the way crimes of violence against women are so often dismissed with crude commonplaces: 'No woman can be raped against her will'; 'she was asking for it'; 'if you're going to be raped, you might as well relax and enjoy it'. She quotes, to telling effect, a (female) character in *Rabbit Redux*, a novel by the highly respected John Updike, who remarks dismissively, 'You know what a rape usually is? It's a woman who changed her mind afterward.'

Unfortunately, this legitimate, urgently necessary insistence that rape is, indeed, a serious and violent crime, was distorted by some later feminists. For another American, Catherine McKinnon, woman is always, indeed almost by definition, a victim. 'To be about to be raped is to be gender female in the process of going about life as usual', she insists.

> You grow up with your father holding you down and covering your mouth so another man can make a horrible searing pain between your legs. When you are older, your husband ties you to a bed and drips hot wax on your nipples and brings in other men to watch and makes you suck his penis . . . In this thousand years of silence, the camera is invented and pictures are made of you while these things are being done . . .

Her friend Andrea Dworkin argued that 'pornography is the law for women', and flatly, without any qualification, equated rape and sexual intercourse. As, indeed, did McKinnon, who from the opening paragraph of *Only Words* (1995) offers a terrible paradigm of what she sees as female experience: a primal paternal rape that freezes us in a state of permanent terror. She constantly evokes the image of a once-violated child who can never grow up, who, she insists, lives on in most women, even those who claim to enjoy consensual sex: 'the aggressor gets an erection; the victim screams and struggles and bleeds and blisters and becomes five years old'. This is melodrama masquerading as feminism.

Chapter 10
Feminists across the world

'Sisterhood is powerful' was one of the most popular feminist slogans in the 1960s and 1970s. But the phrase has been questioned, and sometimes contested, both at the time, and ever since. As the black American poet Audre Lorde argued in 1983, it glosses over

> difference of race, sexuality, class and age . . . Advocating the mere tolerance of difference between women is the grossest reformism. It is a total denial of the creative function of difference in our lives.

Her concerns were echoed in 1995 by Ien Ang, an Australian of Chinese descent, who suggested that the inevitable moments of failure of communication between feminists

> should be accepted as the starting point for a more modest feminism, one which is predicated on the fundamental *limits* to the very idea of sisterhood . . . we would gain more from acknowledging and confronting the stubborn solidity of 'communication barriers' than from rushing to break them down in the name of an idealised unity.

Both writers believe that white middle-class women often seem to be dictating a feminism that concentrates on gender discrimination, while tending to overlook, for example, the class differences and racial discrimination that complicate ideas about gender. Brazilian women have argued that feminism is 'eurocentric', that it has nothing to say to them about urgent local problems: racial violence and health issues, as well as the difficulties black women may encounter when looking for work. Indeed, some Latin American women actually reject the word 'feminism'.

There is also an increasing recognition that, whereas Western feminists have struggled against sexism, and against social and political inequalities, women in the 'Third World' have had to confront additional, and even more intractable, problems. They often have to combat sexism in the form of deep-rooted local beliefs and practices, to do with class, caste, religion, and ethnic biases. In some countries, their battle with these issues has been combined with, and sometimes complicated by, a struggle for the establishment of democratic government and for the most basic freedoms.

But the lives of women in Latin America, Africa, and parts of Asia and the Middle East have also been profoundly affected by colonialism and neocolonialism. 'First World' countries – beginning with Britain and the rest of Europe in the 17th century, followed by the United States from the 19th century onwards – brought vast swathes of the world under their direct control; subjugating local peoples politically and economically. And at the beginning of the 21st century, the United States, by reason of its military, economic, and cultural power, practises a 'discursive colonization' of much of the world.

The term 'Third World' is widely used in contemporary feminist and postcolonial studies; but it is fraught with difficulties. Chandra Talpade Mohanty, for instance, defines it geographically: 'the nation-states of Latin America, the Caribbean, Sub-Saharan Africa, South and South-East Asia, China, South Africa, and Oceania'; she also includes black, Asian, Latino, and indigenous peoples living in the 'West'. But the phrase is sometimes seen as a pejorative label, implying 'underdeveloped' or 'undemocratic' when used by Westerners. Some references to 'Third World women' are, indeed, a 'polite' way of saying 'women of colour', implying a native 'other' in contrast to the 'norm' of Western feminism, and it is sometimes considered more 'correct' these days to talk of 'postcolonial feminism'. But either term may serve as a useful reminder to Westerners of how little we know about the reality of these women's lives, and the way they may be complicated by deep-rooted local beliefs, by practices arising out of class differences, caste, religion, ethnic origins; and also by the legacy of colonialism.

In Latin America, for example, Spanish and Portuguese occupation – as well as slavery – has left profound ethnic and class inequalities, and local feminists may have to struggle with the entrenched patriarchy of the Roman Catholic Church, in addition to the regionally specific male sexist attitudes termed 'machismo'. (Their lives may be complicated further by the equally damaging female equivalent, 'hembrismo' – extreme female submission to male dominance.)

Nevertheless, feminism has a long and fascinating history in some Latin American countries. In Mexico, for example, the 'first wave' of feminism was born during the revolution against the hated dictatorship of President Porfirio Diaz, a bitter struggle that continued between 1910 and 1918. Women took an active part in the struggle. *Solderas* established camps, foraged for food, cooked, and looked after the wounded; but there were also female soldiers, who actively took up arms. Some, dressed in skirts and their best jewellery, followed the men into battle. Others were accused becoming masculine, 'both inwardly and outwardly', though it was admitted that a woman could 'at the hour of combat prove with weapon in hand that she was no longer a *soldera* but a soldier'.

Women intellectuals also supported the revolution; the most influential was Hermila Galindo de Topete, who founded and edited the magazine *Mujer Moderna* [Modern Woman], which fought for sex education in schools, women's suffrage, and the right to divorce. She argued that the Catholic Church was a major obstacle to the advance to feminism in Mexico. Knowing she had no hope of being elected, but wanting to publicize the fact that women wanted and needed the vote, she became the first woman to run for a seat in the Chamber of Deputies. After a prolonged struggle for suffrage, equal civil rights were granted to women in 1927; but it was not until 1952 that they were finally allowed to vote. During the 1970s, the *Movemento de Liberacion de la Mujer* emerged in Mexico as in so many other countries; its members concentrated on the need for legal abortion, increased sentencing for rapists, and help for battered women. And they held frank, and potentially explosive, sexual discussions, amongst other issues questioning the 'tyranny' of the vaginal orgasm.

In Puerto Rica, which had been invaded and occupied by the United States in 1898, a women's movement worked for decades to improve education, as a first step towards other reforms. Universal suffrage was finally granted there in 1936; and most Latin American countries gave women the right to vote in the 1950s. It was a crucial step, but (as Western women had learned earlier) it did not immediately translate into significant changes in women's status and circumstances. Latin Americans in the 1970s and 1980s still had to tackle a wide range of urgent problems. Women's movements argued for full, equal legal and political rights for women, but they were equally concerned with the problem of widespread female illiteracy, and particularly with the miserable circumstances of thousands of women living in shanty towns and slums. Many country women had migrated to the cities, where they became part of a 'sub-proletariat', taking underpaid, temporary jobs as servants (maids, laundresses, cooks) or scraping a living by selling goods on the streets. But women living in the shanty towns often organized to improve their immediate situation: setting up residents' associations and communal kitchens, as well as consumers' organizations and human rights groups. Poverty, poor health care, and botched abortions contributed to a high maternal death rate. (It has been estimated that in Bolivia, there are 390 maternal deaths for every 100,000 births; in Peru, 265.) In some Latin American countries, abortion is forbidden, even when it is necessary to save the mother's life. But Peru, in spite of an authoritarian government, created a Ministry of Women and a Public Defender for women, and laws were passed against domestic violence.

From the 1970s onwards, in São Paulo for example, there was a new concentration on health issues; women were taught how to sterilize water, and how to identify and take preventive action against common childhood diseases. Contraceptive advice was made available; groups were formed to offer mutual support, to set up cooperative schemes within communities; and to campaign for better housing. In the 1980s, a Rural Women Workers Movement was founded by women in the *sertão*, the poor and semi-arid backlands in northeast Brazil. Working as agricultural labourers at half male pay, they fought to be included in drought relief programmes. And they managed to raise the funds to attend the United Nations women's conference in Beijing in 1995.

The Brazilian constitution of 1988 is impressive on paper, amongst other things guaranteeing equal wages, giving women generous maternity leave, and setting minimum wages. But – because most women had little idea of how to obtain their rights – an organization called *Themis* was founded to educate women. They went on to set up a pilot project with a women's police station that handled only cases of rape and violence, which was rapidly followed by similar centres. Also, since 1975, there has been a National Street Children's Movement, as well as women's groups, like *Sempre Viva*, that try to reach and offer medical, educational, and legal help to the millions of children living rough, who are vulnerable to sexual abuse, and are often mistreated by the police. Moreover, black women in Brazil have become more vocal about issues that bear particularly hard on them: racial violence of various kinds, public health policies, and discrimination in the labour market.

In 1975, the United Nations held an International Women's Year Conference in Mexico City, which brought together feminists from all over the world. And since 1981, women from all over Latin America and the Caribbean have been meeting every three years at *encuentros* (encounters), 'to build solidarity, devise innovative forms of political praxis, and elaborate discourses that challenge gender-based and sexual oppression'. Meetings have been held in a different country each year: Colombia, Peru, Brazil, Mexico, Argentina, El Salvador, and Chile. The Left, some women felt, had tended to dismiss feminism as bourgeois and an imperialist import; while the Right and the Church had fought it as a threat to Christian family values. Debates at the *encuentros* were often heated. Like other Latin feminists, participants were interested in equal rights and economic redistribution. But they also discussed controversial issues which, they felt, were usually ignored: domestic violence, sexual harassment, marital rape. In fact, some Latin American feminists believe that their most important achievement is the passage of laws punishing violence against women. In Brazil, for example, women's groups put pressure on the government to fund a Women's Defence Council, which persuaded the Superior Court to overrule a male jury that acquitted a man of killing his wife on the grounds that 'in such crimes what is defended is not honour, but self-adulation, arrogance, and the pride of a man who considers his wife to be his property'.

Over the years, *encuentro* organizers have struggled to involve grass-roots groups, to include as many women as possible (on the grounds that any woman who considered herself a feminist *was* a feminist). Through the early 1990s, they established links abroad, while feminists all over Latin America worked to bring women together for debate and discussion prior to the 1995 Beijing Global Conference on women. Like feminists in other countries, the Latin American organizers had to tackle problems about inclusion and exclusion; and had to accept that inequalities of class, race, and sexual orientation are central to – and complicate – any feminist analysis. Black women from 16 Latin American and Caribbean countries met together to prepare a document for the Beijing Conference.

By the end of the century, younger women, some formerly student activists, others emerging from university feminist programmes, were increasingly attracted to the movement, and were often, perhaps naturally, critical of their elders. They attacked the formerly ground-breaking idea of acknowledging, even celebrating, 'diversity'; that was a crude kind of pluralism, they argued, as often as not implying acceptance of inequality, not allowing true 'recognition or legitimation of others and their experience'.

But international conferences could highlight differences and resentments as well as connections. At a world conference in 1980, some women complained that discussions on veiling, and on female genital surgery, never consulted those women most concerned. At another conference on population and development held in Cairo in 1994, Third World women complained that the agenda had been hijacked by European and American women who were only interested in contraception and abortion; and that when they did tackle 'Third World' issues, they sounded both patronizing and racist. Even at Beijing in 1995, there were complaints that endless discussion by Westerners of reproductive rights and sexual orientation meant that the urgent concerns of women from less developed nations were ignored. As one woman remarked, applying Western feminism to the concerns of, say, South America, 'is not unlike trying to cure severe stomach ache with a pill meant for headaches'.

The problem of cross-cultural misunderstanding is a persistent one. In 1915 an English suffragist called Grace Ellison visited Turkey and wrote a book called *An English Woman in a Turkish Harem*. She displays real understanding of how reforms were affecting women's lives, and how even men seemed to favour some degree of female emancipation. She was deeply interested, too, in the ongoing debate about the wearing of traditional dress. But like many feminist

16. Anti-female circumcision poster, Sudan.

Africa

The problems of Africa are particularly complex. 'African women have always defined and carried out their own struggles ... [it] dates far back in our collective past', argues Amina Mama. Different women are oppressed differently: feminism must acknowledge 'differences of race, class and culture'. Feminism in Africa is heterosexual, pronatal, and concerned with 'bread, butter and power' issues. Genital mutilation, as a way of suppressing unruly female sexuality, is still carried out in some African countries. It is not an inherently Muslim practice, but has become part of the anti-woman stance adopted by certain fundamentalists.

In Nigeria in 2000, a 30-year-old Muslim, Amina Lawal, was condemned by a sharia court to be stoned to death after she had a baby outside marriage – she had apparently been raped. The issue received worldwide coverage because, ironically, the Miss World beauty contest was to be held in Nigeria. Various contestants protested: a few flatly refused to participate; others claimed that they at least intended to speak out against the ruling. A fashion writer's comment that the Prophet Mohammed might well have chosen one of the contestants as his wife led to riots; militant Islamic groups described the contest as a 'parade of nudity' which would promote promiscuity and Aids. But many local women found the courage to demonstrate in angry protest.

theorists since her day, she tended to romanticize traditional customs and the veil, and more than half-regretted the growing number of women wearing Western clothes, at least at home. But when her Turkish friend, a woman called Zegreb Hamun, visited

17. Women protest against the death sentence of the Nigerian Amina Lawal, 2003.

her in England, the tables were neatly, and comically, turned on Ellison. Hamun also published a book of her letters to Ellison, called *A Turkish Woman's European Impressions*. She dismissed a London Ladies' Club as dull and apathetic, lacking the 'mystery and charm' of the harem. But a visit to the Houses of Parliament left her sharply critical:

> But my dear, why have you never told me that the Ladies' Gallery is a harem? A harem with its latticed windows! The harem of the Government! . . . You send your women out unprotected all over the world, and here in the workshop where your laws are made, you cover them with a symbol of protection!

Some recent Western academic feminists theorize endlessly and not very helpfully about the veil and the harem; they seem to deconstruct in order to glamorize, and indulge in their own curious version of 'orientalizing' fantasy. Veiling has certainly been, and remains, an important, and occasionally controversial, issue in some Muslim societies. In 1923, Hudu Sha'rawi, the wife of a well-known Egyptian politician, had caused a sensation when she returned from a trip abroad and publicly removed her veil, though she kept her head covered. But much more importantly, she went on to set up women's groups that fought for better education, the right to vote and run for office, and for reforms concerning the family. Like women since, whether in Egypt or other Muslim countries, she was trying to establish a specifically Islamic feminism.

Five years later, a Lebanese woman, Naxira Zain as Din, published a book arguing that the 'veil is an insult to men and women', and arguing that the oppression of women could not be justified by appeals to Islam. (Religious scholars incited demonstrations against her book.) On the other hand, many women have argued that the veil can be liberating; that it allows them to observe, rather than be observed, not only freeing them from the vagaries of fashion but helping them avoid sexual harassment. It is, of course,

18. A Sundanese Muslim girl displays her inked finger, proof of having voted. Sundanese women were enfranchised in 1964.

impossible to lump all Islamic nations together; moreover, in most Muslim countries (contemporary Egypt is a good example) there are considerable and very visible differences between classes, but also between those women who live in the country and those in the great cities like Cairo and Alexandria. Many Muslim women, especially in big cities, are comfortable unveiled. On the other hand, some Turkish women, for example, have argued that it is in fact the veil that makes it possible for them to enter public life, that gives them the freedom to work, confidently, as teachers or doctors. Arguments occasionally arise in Muslim communities in the West. Schoolgirls in France protested bitterly when they were forbidden to wear headscarves. In England, one Muslim schoolgirl made newspaper headlines when she insisted on wearing, not simply a headscarf and long, loose trousers, but a robe reaching to the ground. But that seems to have been an isolated case; any morning on London streets a few girls heading for school can be seen wearing exactly that.

Problems are more acute in the Muslim theocracies. Saudi Arabia is an extreme example, with its heavy and compulsory veiling of women, who cannot even walk on the street unless accompanied by a male relative, and need male permission to travel and work. Iran, on the other hand, has a long history of women taking independent political action. Even in the 19th century, there were women who wrote eloquently about what they described as the pitiful state of many Iranian women; one issued a pamphlet titled *The Shortcomings of Men*. In the early 20th century, women as well as men demanded constitutional, as well as gender, rights; and women were among the strikers who sought sanctuary at the British embassy in 1906. But their activism was ignored, and in the new constitution of 1906, they were barred from politics and informed that 'women's education and training should be restricted to raising children, home economics and preserving the honour of the family'. But schools for girls were established, and women's associations flourished; in 1911 a book by an Egyptian activist, Ghassem Amin's *Freedom of Women*, was translated into Persian – and was bitterly attacked by the religious authorities. In 1931, women won the right to ask for divorce under certain conditions; in the next decade, a national education system was established, for girls as well as boys; and in 1936, the first women students attended Tehran University, and by 1978 women made up 33% of the workforce. In 1962, women finally won the right to vote, and to stand for office. In Kuwait, women finally gained the vote and the right to stand for office in 2005.

Iranian women were active during the Islamic Revolution of 1978, and various women's organizations were formed. But since that time, official attitudes to women have hardened. In 1979, Ayatollah Khomeini insisted that Iranian women working for the government wear the veil, dismissed women judges, repealed a family protection law, in effect denying women the right to divorce, and banned contraception and abortion. Women could be flogged and fined if they refused to comply with a strict dress code; married women had to get their husband's consent before taking a job. Custody laws were passed that denied mothers rights over their children. But even in those dark days, women's education was not very different to men's; women could still vote, become members of parliament and hold political office, and work outside the home. In 1998, women made up 52% of Iranian university students.

At the same time, many women found their lives more difficult after the Revolution; it was more difficult for women to initiate divorce or to obtain custody of their children; and the minimum age for marriage for girls was lowered first to 13, and then to 10. Women could only acquire a passport with the written consent of their fathers or husbands. Wearing the veil became obligatory; though some women still welcomed the veil as symbol of their rejection of a secular, Westernized lifestyle.

Some secular feminists left the country; others demonstrated against the new order on International Women's Day 1979; still others rejected the imposition of strict dress codes. Dissent was effective and widespread because it was often informal; spread through Xeroxed leaflets and pamphlets, wall newspapers, debates on the streets, women's magazines. Though feminism was forced underground, by the mid-1990s upper- and middle-class women, at least, were again becoming more politically assertive.

Recent women's rights activists have bitterly criticized the fact it is still much more difficult for women to obtain a divorce, and the fact that a father has legal custody of his sons after the age of 2 and of his daughters after the age of 7. Moreover, stoning is still a legal punishment in Iran, and women argue that it is used against their sex much more often than against men. In 2000, a woman accused of adultery and of murdering her husband in collaboration with her lover was sentenced to death by stoning. Another woman, accused of acting in pornographic films and having sex outside marriage, was stoned to death in a Tehran prison. There are reports that prisoners are often raped, and even tortured.

Some feminists have argued that the present relationship between the sexes in Iranian theocracy is in fact totally 'un-Islamic'. Islam, they argue, has traditionally respected women, and allowed them dignity. Many Muslim women insist that the Qur'an has always allowed women, not simply personal dignity, but significant economic rights. It is subsequent interpretation that has often been biased in favour of men. Nor are the sharia, the laws ordained by Allah to guide human behaviour, in essence hostile to women. Some Muslim feminists cite the prophet's wife, Khadija, who, tradition has it, was older than her husband, and an independent and forceful character who first employed him as her trade representative, then insisted that they marry.

Other feminists have argued for separation of religion and the state. But rather than appealing to *human* rights, as most Western feminists have done, many groups within the region have struggled

19. Protest by a women's rights group in Jakarta, November 2000.

to define a specifically Islamic feminism, one that is rooted in local cultures and traditions that, they argue, have always treated women with respect. They have maintained their position in the face of considerable, and perhaps growing, opposition.

Women in Russia and Eastern Europe are often dismissive of Western feminism, and certainly insist that their own history of activism owes little or nothing to the West. In Russia, for example, women have a long and distinctive tradition of activism. In the 1870s, a group of socialist students and workers, who called themselves the Tchaikowsky circle, included many women and argued that it was only when capitalist exploitation was at an end that women would escape the 'double oppression' of housework and factory work. Some women joined, or were active in, a terrorist group called 'Narodnaya Volya' that attacked Tsarist oppression. Many women who were active in a series of strikes in Moscow in 1875 were arrested; their trial received great publicity. As one journalist wrote, a shade sentimentally:

132

an astonished public could look upon the radiant faces of these young women, who with their sweet child-like smiles, were on their way to a place with no return, without hope ... The people said to themselves, 'we are back in the epoch of the early Christians'.

After the 1905 Revolution, many women became involved in a struggle to win the right to vote in elections to the Duma, though historians have argued that this mass movement of women was soon split between those primarily concerned with class struggle, and the so-called 'bourgeois' feminists who were more interested in 'gender oppression'. A Working Women's Mutual Assistance Association was set up in 1907 (men were allowed to join); it tried to reach out to working-class women, and encourage them to join trade unions and the Social Democratic Party.

At an International Conference of Socialist Women, held in Stuttgart in 1907, Clara Zetkin put forward a resolution urging socialists to fight for universal suffrage, which she saw as a step towards ending class struggle. She remarked that, for working women, the right to vote is

> a weapon in the battle which they must wage for humanity to overcome exploitation and class rule. It allows them a greater participation in the struggle for the conquest of political power on the part of the proletariat with the aim of going beyond the capitalist order and building the socialist order, the only one that allows for a radical solution to the women's question.

Activists organized meetings, and tried to encourage working-class women to participate in conferences and actions. On 19 March 1911, the first international women's day had been held in Germany, with thousands of women joining in meetings and marches; in 1913, it was celebrated in Russia as well.

It is sometimes claimed that it was a 1917 women's day demonstration in St Petersburg – they were demanding 'bread and peace' – that touched off the Revolution. But some Russian feminists argue that the Bolshevik Revolution was little direct help to women; that too many men, and some women, insisted that women's interests were identical with men's, and the two must not be separated. After the Revolution, women had better access to education, and were expected to work at full-time jobs. Though cafeterias, laundries, and day care centres were opened in the cities, women still seem to have been expected to take on a heavy double burden. In the 1920s, Alexandra Kollontai emerged as one of the most thoughtful, eloquent, and lastingly interesting writers on women's issues.

After the dissolution of the Soviet Union in 1991, some women, at least, were glad to retreat back into the home; and, though women may have lost out during the transition to capitalism, some have welcomed the chance to become full-time mothers and housewives.

Feminists have recently begun to recognize and explore the problems facing those women from the poorer and less developed parts of the world who travel to the affluent Western countries to work. Women from Mexico and Latin America move to the United States; women from Russia and Eastern Europe look for jobs in Western Europe and in Britain. Algerians and Moroccans go to France; others travel from Sri Lanka. South East Asian girls often seek work in the Middle East – Bahrain, Oman, Kuwait, Saudi Arabia. Some are legal immigrants; those who are not are particularly vulnerable. Many women work as au pairs, maids, nannies, cleaners, do unskilled jobs in old people's homes and hospitals, or take low-waged work in restaurants; but many others, inevitably, drift into prostitution or are trapped in brothels. Filipina women have often been recruited as 'mail-order' brides, usually for men in the United States or Japan.

Some Western women, having fought for women's right to take jobs outside the home, and struggled to achieve their own 'liberation' from domestic drudgery, look for not-too-expensive help with

Alexandra Kollontai

In 1909 the Russian Alexandra Kollontai published a book called *The Social Basis of the Woman Question*, arguing that feminism was not just a matter of political rights, or rights to education and equal pay; the real problem was the way the family was organized and imagined. In 1920 she published *Towards a History of the Working Women's Movement in Russia*, which insisted that women must fight on two fronts. They should reject the growing number of Westernized middle-class women's organizations, which either concentrated on legal equality and the franchise, or saw feminism as a matter of 'free love'. Equally, they must resist the Russian labour movement and the social democrats, who ignored women's specific problems and oppressions, dismissing feminism as inherently 'bourgeois' because it advanced women's interests only within an inherently unjust capitalist society.

Primarily a theorist, Kollontai sometimes responded with real feeling to individuals: for example, to a woman who was desperately unhappy with a husband who drank heavily and forbade her to work. And in one oddly touching Utopian essay, she imagines life as it might be in 1970: a festival on what had once been Christmas Day, as a commune celebrates the fulfilling life they have managed to create together.

domestic work. For some foreign women – the lucky ones – migration is a way of improving their lives. But more often, migrant workers – often unqualified, sometimes barely speaking the language of their new home – get poorly paid, insecure jobs, that leave them isolated and unprotected in all kinds of ways. They often have no idea of what their rights might be – or how to demand them if they do. They rarely have any kind of support network, though in America some campaigning groups have sprung up to their defence. Their very existence poses Western feminists with a painful paradox; they challenge us to look more closely at how we may be conniving in the oppression of other women.

Afterword

So what is the future, or even, *is* there a future, for feminism? Is it, at least in the affluent West, needed any longer? In 1992 the American Susan Faludi argued cogently, and in chilling detail, that feminists have been experiencing what she terms a 'backlash', with women who had undoubtedly benefited from the movement – as well as men, who had perhaps also benefited, though they rarely acknowledged the fact – anxiously remarking that it had all gone too far. As Juliet Mitchell and Ann Oakley suggested in their third collection of essays, *Who's Afraid of Feminism? Seeing Through the Backlash*, feminism makes many people uncomfortable, in part because the 'whole subject of who women are and what they want challenges our division between public and private life'.

In the 20th century, 'first-wave' feminists had demanded civil and political equality. In the 1970s, 'second-wave' feminism concentrated on, and gave great prominence to, sexual and family rights for women. It is these demands, now, that have become the main target of reaction. 'The personal is the political' was a popular 1970s slogan that some contemporary feminists seem to want to reverse. The political is reduced to the *merely* personal, to questions of sexuality and family life – which, of course, also have political implications which still, and urgently, need to be considered..

Natasha Walter, in *The New Feminism* (1998), while admitting that women are 'still poorer and less powerful than men', argues that the task for contemporary feminism is to 'attack the material basis of economic and social and political inequality'. An important point – but she remains extremely vague about precisely what that attack would imply. In one interview, she remarked, as if she had come up with a new idea instead of one that had been around for decades, that 'we want to work with men to change society and not against men': 'After all, especially if things are to change in the domestic arena, that's about men taking on a fair share of domestic work as about women moving more and more out of the home.' Or again, 'we must join hands with one another and with men to create a more equal society'.

But if at one moment she criticizes the older movement for being too personal, a few pages later Walter remarks that it was too political – or, even worse, that its members were 'humourless or dowdy or celibate'. (That is certainly not the way I remember it.) She goes on to describe Margaret Thatcher as 'the great unsung heroine of British feminism', who normalized female success. But Thatcher had no interest whatsoever in women's concerns, and was notoriously unsupportive of other women politicians.

Germaine Greer's *The Whole Woman* (1999) was written partly in angry and effective response to Natasha Walter's book and its 'unenlightened complacency'. Walter, Greer argues, assumes that feminism is all about 'money, sex and fashion'. Though, she adds:

> it was not until feminists of my own generation began to assert with apparent seriousness that feminism had gone too far that the fire flared up in my belly. When the lifestyle feminists had gone just far enough, giving them the right to 'have it all', i.e. money, it would have been inexcusable to remain silent.

People are undoubtedly alarmed by the *threat* of personal change, as much as by change itself. So some cling, nostalgically, to an imaginary golden age of fixed gender identities, the dream of a relationship between a man and a woman, that, whatever its inequities, was comfortably predictable. On the other hand, others insist – in Naomi Wolf's vivid phrase – that there has been a 'genderquake', with more women than ever in powerful positions. Women, Wolf argues in *Fire with Fire* (1983), must give up what she styles 'victim' feminism, stop complaining, and embrace 'power' feminism. But, as Lynne Segal remarks, movingly, at the end of her 1999 *Why Feminism?*, the movement's most radical goal has yet to be realized :

> a world which is a better place not just for some women, but for all
> women. In what I still call a socialist feminist vision, that would be a
> far better world for boys and men, as well.

The long, and at times radically innovative, history of feminism is all too easily forgotten. When 'second-wave' feminism emerged in the late 1960s, it seemed, at the time at least, unexpected, surprising, exciting. One big difference during the years since then has been the way Western women have become much more aware of other feminisms – not just in Europe, but across the world – that, hopefully, may challenge our cherished ideas and certainties, and undermine any complacency that we may have developed.

That wider awareness is due to a number of factors. Technical advances are certainly important: the fact, for example, that feminists in different countries can now communicate quickly and effectively, share experiences and information with large numbers of people, through the Internet. Academic feminism has played an important role in this. A great many universities, certainly in most Western countries, now run courses on women's studies, and specifically on feminism. Academic research has given us extremely valuable insights into women's lives at other times and in other cultures; inviting us to think about differences, as well as about common causes. Academic theses, scholarly articles and texts, as well as conferences, have all helped disseminate important information about feminism across the world.

But there is perhaps a loss involved, which is not often addressed or even acknowledged. I often recall, affectionately, the remark by Rebecca West that I quoted at the opening of this book:

> I myself have never been able to find out precisely what feminism is. I only know that people call me a feminist whenever I express sentiments that differentiate me from a doormat or a prostitute.

All previous feminisms have had an air of excitement, of transgression, or of risk about them: sometimes the excitement of the pioneer, sometimes of the outsider challenging convention. More recently, perhaps, there has been, in addition, the excitement of rediscovering our past, but also – and therefore – of *re-inventing* something. In the late 1960s and the 1970s, women's liberation *was* exciting. We felt that we were 'making it new', that we were exploring both past and present, committing ourselves to something that was new and radical and adventurous. But the girls I talked to recently have never had any comparable experience. They seem uninterested in feminism, partly because they see it simply as an academic subject – something fed to them, which they need not discover for themselves – and it is therefore respectably dull. (Except, of course, for the high-flyers who themselves aspire to academic jobs.) Feminism has, as it were, been spoon-fed to this younger generation of women, so, perhaps naturally and even healthily, they have a sneaking yearning to be politically 'incorrect'. Rejecting academic feminism, at least, seems one way of moving forward. Re-inventing feminism in terms of their own experience may, in the long run, prove another.

But the other difficulty – and it seems to me a crucial one – is that academic feminism has developed a language that makes sense only to a closed circle of initiates. Too many women feel shut out, alienated. This is not only true of feminism, of course; this morning as I was writing this, I opened the newspaper to find an exhilarating attack by the journalist Robert Fisk on what he calls the 'preposterous', even 'poisonous', language so often used by academics in general; used even, perhaps especially, by those who address urgently important political issues. 'University teachers . . . are great at networking each other but hopeless at communicating with most of the rest of the world, including those who collect their rubbish, deliver their laundry and serve up their hash browns.' He ends by jokingly quoting a famous remark by Winston Churchill: 'This is English up with which I will not put.' It would be all too easy to make the same case specifically against academic feminism.

Fisk's point is one that we ignore at our peril. If feminism is to be something living and evolving, it will have to begin by re-inventing the wheel – which in this case means finding not just new issues, but a new language. In spite of everything, I still have faith that feminism *will* take us by surprise again, that it will re-invent itself, perhaps in unforeseen ways, and in areas we have thought little about. It will almost certainly come from outside the academy, and will probably – hopefully – challenge us in ways that, as yet, we cannot even glimpse.

References

Chapter 1

Hildegarde of Bingen, *Selected Writings*, tr. Mark Atherton
(Harmondsworth: Penguin Books, 2001), especially pp. 163–226.

The Book of Margery Kempe, tr. and ed. Barry Windear
(Harmondsworth: Penguin Books, 1986).

Elizabeth Spearing, *Medieval Writings on Female Spirituality*
(Harmondsworth: Penguin Books, 2002); for Julian of Norwich, see
pp. 175–206 (especially p. 201, on the motherhood of God).

Margaret L. King, *Women of the Renaissance* (Chicago and London:
University of Chicago Press, 1991).

Stephanie Hodgson Wright (ed.), *Women's Writing of the Early Modern
Period, 1588-1688* (Edinburgh: Edinburgh University Press, 2002);
see especially 'Jane Anger: her protection for women, 1589', pp. 2–6;
Aemilia Lanyer, 'Salve Deus Rex Judaeorum, 1611', pp. 20–1, and also
pp. 22–77; Anna Trapnel, pp. 212–17.

Keith Thomas, 'Women and the Civil War Sects', *Past and Present*, 13
(1958).

Elaine Hobby (ed.), *Virtue of Necessity: English Women's Writing,
1649-88* (Ann Arbor: University of Michigan Press, 1989) is an
invaluable collection; she includes extracts from Jane Anger, Aemilia
Lanyer, and Anna Trapnel.

H. N. Brailsford, *The Levellers and the English Revolution* (London:
The Cresset Press, 1961), especially p. 119 and pp. 316–17.

On Margaret Fell, see Antonia Fraser, *The Weaker Vessel: Women's Lot in Seventeenth-Century England* (London: Phoenix Press, 1984), pp. 448–60; and Sherrin Marshall-Wyatt, 'Women in the Reformation Era', in *Becoming Visible: Women in European History*, ed. Renate Bridenthal and Claudia Koonz (Boston: Houghton-Mifflin, 1977).

On Eleanor Davis, see Antonia Fraser, *The Weaker Vessel: Women's Lot in Seventeenth-Century England* (London: Phoenix Press, 1984), pp. 188–94.

Chapter 2

Queen Elizabeth, quoted in Stephanie Hodgson Wright (ed.), *Women's Writing of the Early Modern Period, 1588–1688* (Edinburgh: Edinburgh University Press, 2002), p. 1.

Bathsua Makin, quoted in Stephanie Hodgson Wright (ed.), *Women's Writing of the Early Modern Period, 1588–1688* (Edinburgh: Edinburgh University Press, 2002), pp. 287–93. Also see Hilda L. Smith, *Reason's Disciples: Seventeenth-Century English Feminists* (Urbana: University of Illinois Press, 1982).

On Lady Mary Wroth, see *The Poems of Lady Mary Wroth*, ed. Josephine A. Roberts (Baton Rouge: Louisiana State University Press, 1983); and a brief but illuminating comment by Germaine Greer in *Slip-Shod Sibyls* (London: Penguin Books, 1999), pp. 15–16.

On Margaret Cavendish, see Katie Whitaker, *Mad Madge* (London: Chatto and Windus, 2003); and also Dolores Paloma, 'Margaret Cavendish: Defining the Female Self', *Women's Studies*, 7 (1980).

Virginia Woolf, *A Room of One's Own* and *Three Guineas*, with introduction by Hermione Lee (London: Vintage, 2001).

Mary Manley, quoted in Antonia Fraser, *The Weaker Vessel: Women's Lot in Seventeenth-Century England* (London: Phoenix Press, 1984), p. 409.

On Aphra Behn, see Angeline Goreau, *Reconstructing Aphra: A Social Biography of Aphra Behn* (New York: Oxford University Press, 1980); Elaine Hobby (ed.), *Virtue of Necessity: English Women's Writing, 1649–88* (Ann Arbor: University of Michigan Press, 1989), pp. 15–127; and Germaine Greer, *Slip-Shod Sibyls* (London: Penguin Books, 1999), chapters 6 and 7.

Chapter 3

On Mary Astell, see Ruth Perry, *The Celebrated Mary Astell: An Early English Feminist* (Chicago: University of Chicago Press, 1986).

On Mary Wollstonecraft, see *Collected Letters*, ed. Janet Todd (London: Allen Lane, 2003). There are many modern editions of *A Vindication of the Rights of Woman*; I have used the edition with introduction by Miriam Brody (London: Penguin Books, 1992), *Mary* and the unfinished *Maria; Or the Wrongs of Women* (Oxford: Oxford University Press, 1980; or London: Penguin Books, 1992). There are also several good biographies of Wollstonecraft: most recently, Diane Jacobs, *Her Own Woman: The Life of Mary Wollstonecraft* (New York: Simon and Schuster, 2000) and Lyndall Gordon, *Mary Wollstonecraft: A New Genus* (London: Little Brown, 2005).

Chapter 4

Marion Reid, *A Plea for Women* (Edinburgh: Polygon, 1988 [1843]).

Caroline Norton, *English Laws for Women in the Nineteenth Century* [1854]; reprinted as *Caroline Norton's Defense* (Chicago: Academy, 1982).

John Stuart Mill, *The Subjection of Women*, ed. and introduced by Susan M. Okin (Newhaven and London: Yale University Press, 1985).

For Florence Nightingale, see Cecil Woodham Smith, *Florence Nightingale* (London: Penguin Books, 1951; revised edn., 1955); and Nancy Boyd Sokoloff, *Three Victorian Women Who Changed Their World* (London: Macmillan Press, 1982).

For Harriet Martineau, see her *Autobiography*, with Memorials by Maria Weston Chapman (London: Virago, 1983 [1877]); and R. K. Webb, *Harriet Martineau, A Radical Victorian* (London: Heinemann, 1960).

For Frances Power Cobbe, see Barbara Caine, *Victorian Feminists* (Oxford: Oxford University Press, 1992).

Chapter 5

Sheila B. Herstein, *A Mid-Victorian Feminist, Barbara Leigh Smith Bodichon* (Newhaven and London: Yale University Press, 1985):

George Eliot is quoted on p. 71, Mrs Gaskell on p. 80, Elizabeth Barrett Browning on p. 82.

Melanie Phillips, *The Ascent of Woman: A History of the Suffragette Movement and the Ideas Behind It* (London: Little, Brown, 2003), chapter 5.

For Emily Davies, see Margaret Forster, *Significant Sisters: The Grassroots of Active Feminism 1839–1939* (London: Penguin Books, 1986), and also Barbara Caine, *Victorian Feminists* (Oxford: Oxford University Press, 1992), chapter 3.

Jo Manton, *Elizabeth Garrett Anderson: England's First Woman Physician* (London: Methuen, 1965).

On Josephine Butler, see Jane Jordan, *Josephine Butler* (London: John Murray, 2001); and Barbara Caine, *Victorian Feminists* (Oxford: Oxford University Press, 1992), chapter 5.

Roger Manvell, *The Trial of Annie Besant and Charles Bradlaugh* (London: Elek Books, 1976).

Chapter 6

Melanie Phillips, *The Ascent of Woman: A History of the Suffragette Movement and the Ideas Behind It* (London: Little, Brown, 2003), pp. 98–103, 136–9.

Sheila B. Herstein, *A Mid-Victorian Feminist, Barbara Leigh Smith Bodichon* (Newhaven and London: Yale University Press, 1985), pp. 156–69 and chapter VI.

Roger Fulford, *Votes for Women* (London: Faber and Faber, 1957), pp. 33–4.

Florence Nightingale is quoted in Martin Pugh, *The March of the Women: A Revisionist Analysis of the Campaign for Women's Suffrage 1866–1914* (Oxford: Oxford University Press, 2000), p. 55.

Chapter 7

Martin Pugh, *The March of the Women: A Revisionist Analysis of the Campaign for Women's Suffrage 1866–1914* (Oxford: Oxford University Press, 2000) is essential reading: a detailed, scholarly, and thought-provoking account of the prolonged struggle for the vote. Also see Melanie Philips, *The Ascent of Woman: A History of the*

Suffragette Movement and the Ideas Behind It (London: Little, Brown, 2003); and Paul Foot, *The Vote: How It Was Won and How It Was Lost* (London: Viking, 2005) includes a brief but cogent chapter on women's suffrage.

For some memorable (and sometimes witty) examples of the way in which suffragettes expressed their message visually, see the early pages of Liz McQuiston, *Suffragettes and She-Devils: Women's Liberation and Beyond* (London: Phaidon Press, 1997).

See also Emmeline Pankhurst, *My Own Story* (London: Virago, 1979 [1914]) and Sylvia Pankhurst, *The Suffragette Movement* (London: Virago, 1977 [1931]).

Chapter 8

See Sheila Rowbotham, *A Century of Women* (London: Viking, 1997) on Sylvia Pankhurst, and the effects of the war, p. 64 ff.; and Paul Foot, *The Vote: How It Was Won and How It Was Lost* (London: Viking, 2005), especially pp. 232–5, on women and the war.

See also Martin Pugh, *Women and the Women's Movement in Britain 1914–1999* (London: Macmillan Press, 1992), especially chapters 1–6; chapter 3 discusses the birth and decay of the idea of a woman's party; pp. 49–50 and 142–3 discuss the Six Point Group; Rebecca West is quoted on p. 72.

Roger Manvell, *The Trial of Annie Besant and Charles Bradlaugh* (London: Elek Books, 1976).

On Margaret Sanger and Marie Stopes, see Ruth Hall, *Marie Stopes: A Biography* (London: Andre Deutch, 1977). On Stella Browne, see Rowbotham, especially p. 194.

Chapter 9

Simone de Beauvoir, *The Second Sex*, English translation by H. M. Parshley (London: Jonathan Cape, 1953). Her four autobiographical volumes and her novels are also all available in English translation.

bel hooks, *Feminist Theory from Margin to Centre* (Boston: South End Press, 1984).

Germaine Greer, *The Female Eunuch* (London: Paladin, 1971).

Juliet Mitchell, *Woman's Estate* (Harmondsworth: Penguin Books,

1971) is essential reading for the ideas and strategies of 'second-wave' feminism; on consciousness-raising, see pp. 61–3. See also her *Psychoanalysis and Feminism* (London: Allen Lane, 1974) and *Women: The Longest Revolution* (London: Virago, 1984).

Shulamith Firestone, *The Dialectic of Sex* (New York: Morrow, 1970).

Kate Millet, *Sexual Politics* (Garden City, New York: Doubleday, 1970).

Leslie B. Tanner (ed.), *Voices from Women's Liberation* (New York: Signet Books/New American Library, 1971).

Susan Brownmiller, *Against Our Will: Men, Women and Rape* (New York: Bantam, 1976), especially pp. 5, 346, 348; see also Brownmiller's *In Our Time: Memoirs of a Revolution* (London: Aurum Press, 2000), particularly the essay 'Rape is a Political Crime Against Women', pp. 194–224.

Catherine McKinnon, *Only Words* (London: HarperCollins, 1995), pp. 5, 28, 40.

Chapter 10

Audre Lorde, 'The Master's Tools Will Never Dismantle the Master's House', in *This Bridge Called My Back: Writings by Radical Women of Colour*, ed. C. Moraga and F. Anzaldua (New York: Kitchen Table Press, 1983).

Ien Ang, 'I'm a Feminist but . . . ', in *Transitions: New Australian Feminisms*, ed. B. Caine and R. Pringle (Sydney: Allen and Unwin, 1995).

Mai Yaman (ed.), *Feminism and Islam: Legal and Literary Perspectives* (New York: New York University Press, 1996).

Reina Lewis and Sara Mills (eds.), *Feminist Postcolonial Theory: A Reader* (Edinburgh: Edinburgh University Press, 2003); in particular, see Chandra Talpade Mohanty, 'Under Western Eyes', pp. 49–74; and Reina Lewis, 'On Veiling, Vision and Voyage: Cross-Cultural Dressing and Narratives of Identity', pp. 520–41.

'Encountering Latin American and Caribbean Feminisms', Sonia E. Alvarez, Politics Department, University of California at Santa Cruz. CA95064 (*sonia@cats.ucsc.edu*).

Roads to Beijing: Fourth World Conference on Women in Latin America and the Caribbean (Quito: Ediciones Flora Tristan).

Barbara Ehrenreich and Arlie Russell Hochschild (eds.), *Global Women: Nannies, Maids and Sex Workers in the New Economy* (London: Granta Books, 2003).

Afterword

Natasha Walter, *The New Feminism* (London: Virago, 1999).

Naomi Wolf, *Fire with Fire* (London: Chatto and Windus, 1993).

Germaine Greer, *The Whole Woman* (London: Doubleday, 1999).

Further Reading

Christine Bolt, *Feminist Ferment: 'The Woman Question' in the USA and England, 1870–1940* (London: UCL Press, 1995)

John Charvet, *Feminism* (London: Dent, 1982)

Susan Faludi, *Backlash: The Undeclared War Against Women* (London: Chatto and Windus, 1992)

Estelle B. Freedman, *No Turning Back: The History of Feminism and the Future of Women* (London: Profile Books, 2002)

Sarah Gamble (ed.), *The Routledge Companion to Feminism and Postfeminism* (London: Routledge, 2001)

Germaine Greer, *The Female Eunuch* (London: MacGibbon and Kee, 1970)

Germaine Greer, *The Whole Woman* (London: Transworld Publishers, 2000)

Sandra Kemp and Judith Squires (eds.), *Feminisms* (Oxford: Oxford University Press, 1997)

Helena Kennedy, *Eve Was Framed: Women and British Justice* (London: Vintage, 2005)

Anne Koedt, Ellen Levine, and Anita Rapone (eds.), *Radical Feminism* (New York: Quadrangle/The New York Times Book Co., 1973)

Reina Lewis and Sara Mills (eds.), *Feminist Postcolonial Theory* (Edinburgh: Edinburgh University Press, 2003)

Janet Price and Margrit Shildrick (eds.), *Feminist Theory and the Body: A Reader* (Edinburgh: Edinburgh University Press, 1999)

Sheila Rowbotham, *The Past is Before Us: Feminism in Action since the 1960s* (Harmondsworth: Penguin Books, 1990)

Sheila Rowbotham, *A Century of Women: The History of Women in Britain and the United States* (London: Viking, 1997)

Marsha Rowe (ed.), *Spare Rib Reader* (Harmondsworth: Penguin Books, 1982)

Jennifer Mather Saul, *Feminism: Issues and Arguments* (Oxford: Oxford University Press, 2003)

Lynne Segal, *Is the Future Female? Troubled Thoughts on Contemporary Feminism* (London: Virago Press, 1987)

Lynne Segal, *Why Feminism?* (Cambridge: Polity Press, 1999)

Bonnie G. Smith, *Global Feminisms since 1945* (London: Routledge, 2000)

Index

Index

Visit the
VERY SHORT
INTRODUCTIONS
Web site

www.oup.co.uk/vsi

➤ **Information** about all published titles

➤ News of **forthcoming books**

➤ **Extracts** from the books, including titles not yet published

➤ **Reviews** and views

➤ **Links** to other **web sites** and main OUP web page

➤ Information about **VSIs in translation**

➤ **Contact** the editors

➤ **Order** other **VSIs** on-line

Expand your collection of
VERY SHORT INTRODUCTIONS

LITERARY THEORY
A Very Short Introduction
Jonathan Culler

Literary Theory is a controversial subject. Said to have transformed the study of culture and society in the past two decades, it is accused of undermining respect for tradition and truth, encouraging suspicion about the political and psychological implications of cultural products instead of admiration for great literature. In this Very Short Introduction, Jonathan Culler explains 'theory', not by describing warring 'schools' but by sketching key 'moves' that theory has encouraged and speaking directly about the implications of cultural theory for thinking about literature, about the power of language, and about human identity. This lucid introduction will be useful for anyone who has wondered what all the fuss is about or who wants to think about literature today.

'It is impossible to imagine a clearer treatment of the subject, or one that is, within the given limits of length, more comprehensive. Culler has always been remarkable for his expository skills, and here he has found exactly the right method and tone for his purposes.'

Frank Kermode

www.oup.co.uk/vsi/literarytheory

POSTMODERNISM
A Very Short Introduction
Christopher Butler

Postmodernism has become the buzzword of contemporary society over the last decade. But how can it be defined? In this Very Short Introduction Christopher Butler lithely challenges and explores the key ideas of postmodernism, and their engagement with literature, the visual arts, film, architecture, and music. He treats artists, intellectuals, critics, and social scientists 'as if they were all members of a loosely constituted and quarrelsome political party' – a party which includes such members as Jacques Derrida, Salman Rushdie, Thomas Pynchon, David Bowie, and Micheal Craig-Martin – creating a vastly entertaining framework in which to unravel the mysteries of the 'postmodern condition', from the politicizing of museum culture to the cult of the politically correct.

> 'a preeminently sane, lucid, and concise statement about the central issues, the key examples, and the notorious derilections of postmodernism. I feel a fresh wind blowing away the miasma coiling around the topic.'
>
> **Ihab Hassan, University of Wisconsin, Milwaukee**

www.oup.co.uk/isbn/0-19-280239-9

SOCIOLOGY
A Very Short Introduction
Steve Bruce

Drawing on studies of social class, crime and deviance, work in bureaucracies, and changes in religious and political organizations, this Very Short Introduction explores the tension between the individual's role in society and society's role in shaping the individual, and demonstrates the value of sociology as a perspective for understanding the modern world.

> 'Steve Bruce has made an excellent job of a difficult task, one which few practising sociologists could have accomplished with such aplomb. The arguments are provocatively and intelligently presented, and the tone and the style are also laudable.'
> **Gordon Marshall, University of Oxford**

www.oup.co.uk/vsi/sociology

PHILOSOPHY
A Very Short Introduction
Edward Craig

This lively and engaging book is the ideal introduction for anyone who has ever been puzzled by what philosophy is or what it is for.

Edward Craig argues that philosophy is not an activity from another planet: learning about it is just a matter of broadening and deepening what most of us do already. He shows that philosophy is no mere intellectual pastime: thinkers such as Plato, Buddhist writers, Descartes, Hobbes, Hume, Hegel, Darwin, Mill and de Beauvoir were responding to real needs and events – much of their work shapes our lives today, and many of their concerns are still ours.

> 'A vigorous and engaging introduction that speaks to the philosopher in everyone.'
>
> **John Cottingham, University of Reading**

> 'addresses many of the central philosophical questions in an engaging and thought-provoking style ... Edward Craig is already famous as the editor of the best long work on philosophy (the Routledge Encyclopedia); now he deserves to become even better known as the author of one of the best short ones.'
>
> **Nigel Warburton, The Open University**

www.oup.co.uk/isbn/0-19-285421-6